TOGETHER
for
CHRISTMAS 2

a resource anthology

CIO PUBLISHING
Church House, Dean's Yard, London SW1P 3NZ

ISBN 0 7151 0410 1

Published 1982 for the General Synod Board of Education
by CIO Publishing /

Printed in England by The Ludo Press Ltd, London SW18 3DG

CONTENTS

Poems, songs and carols *Page*

Stories

Background

FOREWORD

The first of all the *Together* anthologies to appear was *Together for Christmas*, and since then these collections have gained many friends among all those concerned with the Christian education of children. It is with particular pleasure, therefore, that we present the latest in the series to be concerned with resources for celebrating the Christmas festival and proclaiming its inner meaning.

As old friends will know, the plays, services, songs and stories to be found within these pages have been written by contributors to *Together* magazine, which is produced by the General Synod Board of Education to help all those working with children who wish to swap and share ideas: clergy, day-school and voluntary teachers.

Together is ecumenical in outlook and readership, and contributions from Anglican, Roman Catholic and Free Church readers will be found in this volume. All have been tried out in practice and are presented here for you to present as you will. It is not necessary to write for permission to perform these plays within a school or church setting, but if you bring off a successful production, we should be delighted if you would write and tell us a little about it. Perhaps you, too, may even be moved to contribute to our next anthology.

If you feel that *Together* magazine, with its nine issues a year full of resources, might be of help to you, drop a line to the Circulation Manager, *Together*, 6 Mill Fields, Haughley, Stowmarket, Suffolk IP14 3PU. And don't forget to look out for other *Together* anthologies. We have many more goodies to offer!

Pamela Egan,
Editor, Together

NURSERY-SONG NATIVITY

A play by Jane McInnes, originally written for use with mentally handicapped children and also suitable for First schools

Scene I

> [*Joseph and Mary enter stage right, Joseph supporting Mary. Wander from side to side of stage in front of CLOSED curtains tapping on each wall. At each tap, voice off calls 'No room, no room!' As they come centre stage, Joseph sings 'Joseph's Song' once through.*]

Joseph: Joseph am I,
With Mary I came.
To be taxed, and I am unable
To find somewhere to stay
And so that is why,
Our baby was born in a stable.

> (To be sung by Joseph to 'Little Bo Beep")

> [*The rest of the cast and audience then sing 'Joseph's Song' while Joseph and Mary exit through curtain and take up position (curtains still closed) on stage*].

Scene II

> [*Shepherds enter stage left in front of closed curtains and settle themselves for the night, two lying down and one remaining sitting up on guard. Suddenly Angel appears. Shepherds very frightened. Angel sings his 'Angel's Song'.*]

Angel: Shepherds, don't be frightened.
It's joyful news I bring.
This night there has been born to you
A new and heavenly king.
In Bethlehem you'll find him,

6

To human view displayed.
All safely wrapped in swaddling clothes
And in a manger laid.

> (To be sung by Angel to 'Sing a song of Sixpence')

[*Audience then take up 'Angel's Song' and, while they are sing-ing it, Angel exits. Goes backstage and takes up position behind Mary.*]

Scene III

[*Shepherds recover from their fright and, gathering up their be-longings, turn towards the closed curtain. They quietly open the curtains, one shepherd to each curtain, drawing them back to reveal stable scene. Shepherds sing 'Shepherds' Song'.*]

Shepherds: We are the shepherds
Come from our farms.
Here we find Jesus
In Mary's arms.
Sleep little baby,
Joseph is near.
No one can hurt you,
You've nothing to fear.

> (To be sung by Shepherds to 'Rock a bye baby')

[*Audience then all sing 'Shepherds' Song', while shepherds take up their positions on floor, all kneeling.*]

Scene IV

[*Kings enter slowly from stage right singing 'Three Wise Men'*]

Kings: Three wise men.
Three wise men.
All of them kings,
All of them kings.
Bearing gifts they have travelled afar.
To search for a baby they followed a star.
They gave him some gold, frankincense and some myrrh.
Three wise men.

> (To be sung by the Three Kings to 'Three blind mice')

Caspar: My name is Caspar
  I've come thro' the cold.
  To bring baby Jesus
  A nugget of gold.

(To be sung by 1st King to 'I love little pussy')

Melchior: Melchior's me, I've come
  Many a mile.
  To worship and give
  Frankincense to the child.

(To be sung by 2nd King to 'I love little pussy')

Balthazar: I am Balthazar
  I've come from afar.
  To give to the baby
  My present of myrrh.

(To be sung by 3rd King to 'I love little pussy')

[When each King finishes, audience take up that song, and while they are singing, King moves to his place in the stable.]

[Kings remain standing: Mary picks baby out of manger. Mary then sings 'Mary's Song'.]

Mary: I had a little baby.
  Jesus he is called.
  I've laid him in a manger
  In a cattle stall.
  Wise men from the East have come to visit me,
  All for the sale of my little baby.

(To be sung by Mary to 'I had a little nut tree')

[Audience then sing 'Mary's Song'.]

[Short pause .... everyone remains as still as possible. Then all the cast and audience sing 'Everyone's Song'.]

8

All: Jesus is born
　　　Dilly dilly,
　　　Jesus is born.
　　　Laid in the hay
　　　Dilly dilly,
　　　To keep him warm.
　　　There is the ox
　　　Dilly dilly,
　　　There the wise men
　　　Shepherds and ass,
　　　Dilly dilly,
　　　And so
　　　Amen.

(To be sung by all to 'Lavender's blue')

Note: There is a final song, 'Mary Had a Baby'. which was written for all those who could not manage the more difficult words or who did not have a part in the play. This may be sung at any time before, during or after the play so that everyone in the class will have had a part to play in the production.

All: Mary had a baby, a baby, a baby,
　　　Oh, Mary had a baby
　　　On that first Christmas Day.
　　　They called the baby Jesus,
　　　Called him Jesus, called him Jesus,
　　　They called the baby Jesus
　　　On the first Christmas Day.

(To be sung by all to 'Poor Jenny sits a-weeping')

THE GREAT CHRISTMAS SLIDE SHOW

Shirley Barnes shows that small numbers in a First School need be no bar to an imaginative project

When in the autumn we began to plan for the traditional Nativity Play at the end of term, we realised that we had somehow to solve the problem of making up a cast from only seven children, for that was the total number on roll in our little village school.

Assuming that we kept the cast to the bare minimum, we still needed at least double that number. What could we do?

The children, fairly evenly spaced in age between five and seven years, were quick to volunteer to take more than one part; but then we were faced with the problem of lengthy intervals throughout the play for costume changing.

To cut a long story short, we overcame our problem by making a colour-slide film show of the play. Thereby we gave ourselves the opportunity to take as long as we needed over the costume changes between scenes. This, in turn, released us from the tight schedule of a live stage performance, and allowed us to set up more elaborate scenery than is usually possible on a stage.

We therefore began work in late September to prepare the sets for our film. To make these as authentic as possible involved much research by the children into the country of Palestine and everyday life there in the time of our Lord.

First, we made huge backcloths, about six metres by two-and-a-half metres, out of lengths of wallpaper stuck together, these we painted out in the playground on fine days, using brooms, car-wash brushes, and hand-brushes dipped in bowls and buckets of paint.

We then made the props required. For example, for Mary's house we made oil lamps from clay, loaves from flour and salt dough, fruit from *papier mâché*; and we collected a variety of mats, rugs and earthenware pots, to make the room look really lived in. For the carpenter's workshop we made replicas of tools, and assembled various pieces of wood with which to surround the work-bench.

With the use of an episcope we made cardboard models of Joseph's donkey, the innkeeper's oxen, sheep and lambs, and the wise men's camels, all in correct proportion to the child-sized actors in the play.

The time came to choose the cast. So ambitious had our play become that we required forty-six characters, including the angelic host in the sky and mortal crowds in the streets. Each child, therefore, had at least six parts in the play; and the Welfare Assistant had forty-six costumes to make.

The dramatisation of the story began. We rehearsed a few times with entirely spontaneous dialogue, so that the children got the feel of their parts, and then began the filming. During the filming the children were frequently interrupted to be placed strategically for the camera shots, and then, as they resumed their action, the shots were taken. An SLR 35mm camera was used, with a single flash unit on an extension cable.

When the films were returned from processing, the slides were edited. One hundred and twenty-five were placed in sequence to show: the annunciation; the visit of Mary to her cousin Elizabeth; the angel's appearance to Joseph; the tax decree by Caesar; Mary and Joseph's journey to Bethlehem; the inn and stable; the shepherds on the hillside and their visit to the stable; the journey of the Magi to Bethlehem via Herod's palace; and the consecration of the Holy Baby in the Temple.

The children then recorded a narration of the Christmas story to accompany the colour slides. Finally, they learnt to play on the chime bars, and to sing a song especially composed for the film.

After so much hard work the seven children were thrilled to sit with their parents on the night of the film show and enjoy with them the twenty-five minute performance of 'The Christmas Story'. Perhaps with enjoyment came, too, a greater sense of joy and wonder at the revelation of God's love.

'IT'S A SECRET!'

A Christmas play for children in primary or Sunday school by Anne Shells

Cast

Secret
Candle
Christmas Children
Love Quartet
Fathers and Mothers

Angel
Mary
Elizabeth
Joseph
Shepherds
Kings

'It's a Secret' was written for a primary school where space was limited. The audience (parents and friends) sat round the hall and were involved in the performance. The ideas are adaptable, rehearsal minimal and no scenery is needed except a screen. The play does, however, depend on the part of Secret. This is within the scope of a child but could be better performed by a teacher or the producer, who would then be in command of the children and audience throughout.

Children should wear soft shoes and be encouraged to wear matching-colour T-shirts or sweaters with their trousers or skirts. Their Christmas symbols can be worn on the head or carried, and may be as simple or complicated as wished. The nativity scenes should not be overdressed.

Before the performance begins, the audience are asked to take part in helping the children to 'sit down' and 'get up' by indicating with their arms, following Secret's directions. Emphasis should be made between the quiet and noisy parts (noisy parts not too noisy and quiet parts very quiet). Time of the play is about half an hour.

[*Candle enters from side door with unlighted candle, sits down in middle of the hall.*]

Candle: I am Candle.

[*Secret appears from behind the screen. He (or she) is happy, full of mystery and importance, going about on tip-toe and whispering.*]

Secret: I am Secret. That is my name. Secret? [*He nods*]. Sssh. Yes, Secret. Our play is called: 'It's a Secret', and you'll see what I mean. Will you help to make the children sit down and get up when they are supposed to?

[*He goes behind the screen. Audience whispers 'Secret, secret'. and the unseen Children whisper 'Secret' as well. Children suddenly appear from everywhere (but not all at once) including from among the audience. They are carrying or wearing on their heads various things associated with Christmas, e.g. holly, mistletoe, tree, crackers, ivy, pudding, turkey, presents, stocking, Father Christmas, balloons, etc. They are noisy and shouting. Each announces his identity 'I am Holly' - the last says 'I am Dance and Sing'. They make a circle and dance round to music. Candle is still sitting in the circle.*]

Children: Christmas is coming! Hooray! Hooray!

Secret [*comes out from behind the screen*]: Ssh. SSSSsssssssssh.

Children: Why? What's happened? What? [*They crowd round Secret, who gathers them up in front of the screen.*] What's behind there? What is it? What's there? [*Secret gets one or two children dramatically to move the screen away. There is nothing to be seen.*]

Children: [*disappointed*]: Oh! Oh, there's nothing there.

[*Secret puts the screen back again.*]

Secret: Can you see Christmas? Well, can you? Christmas isn't only crackers. It isn't only cake. It isn't only chocolates. [*He points towards and touches each child in turn and they then sit down. He leaves Candle to the last.*] I need you to help me. You can help me look for Christmas. [*Candle goes behind the screen again, but still nothing there.*] Well, help him to find IT. [*Children all get up and search around aimlessly.*]

Children: What are we looking for?
What are we looking for?
What are we looking for?
What are we looking for?
What are we looking for?
What are we looking for?

Secret: [*enjoying their confusion*]: Well, what *are* you all looking for?

Children: We don't know. You told us to look for Christmas. What *IS* Christmas?

[*Candle shows Secret a Quartet of little children asleep. Secret makes the other children sit down and wakes up the little Quartet. He does a lot more ssh-sshing. Then he lines up the four children and pins on the letters: LOVE.*]

Candle: I'll show you. Now watch.

[*The Quartet nod their heads, smile and look happy.*]

Secret: [*points to the word LOVE*]: Now, go and look for it.

Children: [*get up and wander about aimlessly, grumbling*]: I can't see any. I thought I felt some. Where? Where is it?

[*Secret calls them back and gets them to sit down again. He looks around the audience. Some children return to their parents and sit with them.*]

Secret: Is your mother there? Is your father there? Is your gran? Your teacher? Can you see love? Is it noisy? Aha! You see, it's a quiet thing!

[*Five or six pairs of fathers and mothers enter, carrying their babies. They are singing a lullaby. They stand around the screen. All the children hum the lullaby.*]

'Still, still,
Jesus is here,
Still, still
Angels are near.'   (*Hymns and Songs for Children*, NS/SPCK)

[*Secret and Candle take the screen away. Mary, Joseph and the Baby are seated. They can be put in position during the entrance of fathers and mothers, while attention of audience is elsewhere. A parent or possibly the Vicar or a teacher from among the audience - whoever takes final prayers - stands up.*]

14

Adult: 'When all things were in quiet silence, and night was in the midst of her swift course, then thine Almighty Word, O Lord, stepped down from thy Royal Throne.'

Mothers and Fathers (each say a line in turn):
Love was born on Christmas Day
Love lay on the hay
This Day
His Birthday
Love was born.

[*They group together and stay nearby.*]

All [*sing*]: 'How silently, how silently', verse only, from 'O Little Town of Bethlehem'.

[*By now Secret has made sure the Children are sitting down among the audience, including the little Quartet.*]

Secret: You see, at first it was a secret. Mary was the first person in all the world to have this secret.

[*Mary takes the Baby and gives it to the Love Quartet (or a suitable child) to mind for the time being. Joseph stands to one side. Mary then kneels; an angel comes in and they mime the Annunciation. Background music would be appropriate during the following mimes.*]

Angel: Mary, you are to be the mother of God's Son. And your cousin Elizabeth is going to have a baby too. You may go and tell her your secret.

Secret: God knows that if you have a tremendous secret you must share it with someone. Mary did go and share her secret with Elizabeth.

[*Elizabeth enters and they mime the Visitation.*]

Then the Angel told Joseph the secret, so that when Mary came home they could talk it over together.

[*Joseph and Angel mime this scene, followed by Joseph and Mary talking together.*]

Mary and Joseph now journey to Bethlehem and find the stable.

[*Two children bring in the manger and chair for Mary. The Quartet bring back the Baby. The Lullaby is repeated. Shepherds come in before it is finished, breaking into the quiet. Candle escorts them to the manger.*]

Secret: Ssssh, please be quiet, shepherds, please be quiet.

[*Shepherds kneel, then get up, waving their arms and shouting for joy.*]

Secret: Don't make such a noise. You mustn't tell everyone.

Shepherds: We must, we must, all the world is going to know. Jesus has come to save everyone!

Children: Look! Kings! Wise Men!

[*Candle escorts the Kings to the manger. They kneel with gifts, then leave hurriedly.*]

Mothers and Fathers: They are in a hurry. Herod wants to know the secret.
Herod wants to kill Jesus.
Mary has got to hide him.
Mary and Joseph have got to escape.
They are refugees.
The world doesn't want Jesus.

Secret: But Jesus wants the world.

Candle: He is the Light of the world. [*He lights a candle and lifts it up.*] Jesus loves us all. [*All the children get up and run round the room.*]

Children: Don't forget him on Christmas Day. Don't forget him on Christmas Day. Christmas Day is his day. Jesus is alive. Joy! Happiness!

[*Secret quietens them all down.*]

Secret: Now, all together, children.

Children: Christmas is here. Jesus loves us all, it isn't a secret any more. Let's tell everyone! [*They hold up their arms high and wide.*]

[*The play can end with prayers and a blessing.*]

THE MOST IMPORTANT PART OF CHRISTMAS

A play for a family service, also suitable for a church primary school, planned by Olive Peters and the children of her Sunday group

The following was part of morning worship on the Sunday before Christmas at St George's URC Church, Southport.

At the beginning of Advent, when the project was first mentioned, it was discussed fully with the children. They decided what the 'important' things should be. Those taking part decided for themselves what they should say. The crying of the baby was taped beforehand and played through the amplifier. The singing of 'Still the night', to guitar accompaniment, was also pre-recorded. This was played through the amplifier, the children singing with the sound of their own voices. They sang confidently and there was a good volume of sound to fill the church.

Characters could be varied (e.g. a Parcel) and if it is desired to let more children take part, some could enter in groups, e.g. carol-singers, Christmas decorations, toys.

The scene at the end can be as simple or elaborate as you wish. Ours was a simple, set tableau while the carols were sung. Then the children went to sit in the pews for the remainder of the service. But it could be arranged for instance that the baby is in the manger, with Mary and Joseph standing by, at first. The shepherds can come in and adore, during the singing of an appropriate carol - the Wise Men can follow, and modern-day children if this is wanted.

[*Across a raised part at the front of the church curtains were drawn with a Christmas Tree standing at the left.*]

Leader: What is the most important part of Christmas?

Christmas Tree: [*Child dressed to represent Christmas Tree comes from under the branches of the Tree and stands on a bench close by it.*] I'm the Christmas Tree. I'm the most important part of Christmas.

Leader: The Christmas Tree is very important. We have one in our homes and one in church. Last week, when we brought our presents for the children who won't be getting many this Christmas, we put them at the foot of the tree.

[*By this time Christmas Tree has come into the centre, where he is joined by Father Christmas, bulging sack on his back.*]

Father Christmas: No, I'm the most important part of Christmas. I give presents to everyone.

Leader: The getting and giving of presents is a very important part of Christmas to all of us. So Father Christmas, with his lovely surprises, means a great deal.

[*Plum Pudding enters.*]

Plum Pudding: I'm the Plum Pudding. I'm the most important, because eating is the best part of Christmas.

Leader: At Christmas, we all like to have good food Plum pudding, Christmas cake, mince-pies, turkey - lots of good things to eat and enjoy.

Christmas Cracker [*joining the others*]: No, parties are the best thing at Christmas.

Leader: We like to pull crackers at our Christmas parties. We all get together with our friends at Christmas. We make a special point of seeing members of our family who live away, too. Parties at church, parties at school, parties at home. All the fun of our parties is very important to us.

Carol-singer [*coming down the aisle, singing a verse of 'Away in a manger'*]: Singing carols is the most important part of Christmas.

Leader: We can hardly imagine Christmas without carols. We come to church to sing them each year, we hear them on radio and television and we sing them together in our homes. Carol-singing is very important at Christmas.

[*All start quarrelling and making a noise, saying such things as:*]

'I'm the most important part of Christmas'
'No, it's not you'
'Me, I'm the best'
'You're not', *etc.*

Carol-singer: Stop. Be quiet. Listen.

[*When they are all quiet, the crying of a baby can be heard.*]

Plum Pudding: It's a baby crying.

[*Crying is faded out during next speech.*]

Carol-singer: We were all wrong. A baby's the most important part of Christmas. A very special baby. If Jesus hadn't been born there wouldn't even *be* any Christmas. He's the most important at Christmas and any other time, too.

[*They turn to curtains and draw them back. Tableau of baby in manger, Mary, Joseph and worshipping Shepherds is revealed.*]

Characters [*sing*]: 'Still the night' [or other version of 'Silent Night']

Congregation [*sings*]: 'Come, come, come to the manger'. (*Celebration Hymnal*, published by Mayhew/McCrimmon.)

MARY'S SECRET

A carol service for the younger ones, devised by C. Dixon and given by Langley Park J.M.I. School, Durham

All sing: 'Once in Royal David's City'

Children sing: 'Listen, Listen' (words and music on pages 24 and 25)

Child: To Nazareth, long time ago,
A herald came one day,
He said the folk must listen
To what he had to say.

Chorus [*speech*]: He blew his trumpet loud and clear
And spoke so everyone could hear.

Child (Herald): The emperor commands you all
At once to make your way
Each one to his own city
And none must disobey.

Chorus: He blew his trumpet loud and clear
And spoke so everyone could hear.

Child (Herald): So hurry and get ready
Let there be no delay
For when the emperor commands
No one can say him nay.

For each one must be counted
And each must pay his tax
So everyone make ready
Fill up your bags and packs.

Chorus: He blew his trumpet loud and clear
And spoke so everyone could hear.

20

Child: Then everyone so sadly
Went back home to prepare
To travel to the city
And find a lodging there.

Among them was a lady
And Mary was her name
She with her own man Joseph
Began to do the same.

But Mary had a secret
That she had kept so well
And now she went to Joseph
Her secret for to tell.

Child (Mary): Soon I shall have a baby,
A special baby too,
Please Joseph, will you help me,
This weary journey through?

Child (Joseph): Why yes, my sweetest Mary,
You who are so kind,
Our gentle little donkey
Will carry you, you'll find.

Children sing: 'Little Donkey' (*Carol, Gaily Carol, A & C Black*)

Children sing: 'Here we go up to Bethlehem' (*Carol, Gaily Carol*)

All sing: 'O Little Town of Bethlehem'

Child: The road was long and dreary
The miles dragged slowly by
And when they came to Bethlehem
The stars shone in the sky.

Chorus: The travellers kept plodding on
The journey was so very long.

Child: The town was full of people
No lodging could be found
When Joseph and dear Mary
The city sought around.

Chorus: The travellers kept plodding on
The journey was so very long.

21

Child: At last they met a landlord
Who showed some love and care
And offered them a stable
Though it was cold and bare.

L. Pme

Children sing: 'There isn't any room' (*Carol, Gaily Carol*)

Child: They went inside and shut the door
And brought that stable fame
For Mary's baby boy child
Into the quiet came.

Me.

Chorus: The animals all gathered round
And looked at him without a sound.

Children sing: 'Mary had a Baby Boy' (*Carol, Gaily Carol*)
'Jesus our Brother'
'I, said the donkey' (*Carol, Gaily Carol*)

All sing: 'Still the Night' ('Silent Night')

Child: Out in the fields some shepherds
Heard all about the birth
And came to see the baby,
The dearest child on earth.

Chorus: The animals all gathered round
And looked at him without a sound.

Child: They lovingly looked at the boy
Asleep in manger bare,
Then called the people in the town,
To come and see him there.

Chorus: And all the people came with joy
To welcome Mary's little boy.

Children sing: 'Baby Jesus, sleeping softly' (*Carol, Gaily Carol*)
'Come, see this little stranger' (*Carol, Gaily Carol*)
'Drummer Boy' (*Carol, Gaily Carol*)
'Come with me to Bethlehem' (*Christmas Things to Sing*, Arnolds)

Child: Now in a country far away
Looking up one night,
Some wise men saw a shining star
Making the dark sky light.

Children (Kings): What can it mean, they wondered.
It moves across the sky.
Perhaps a king is born somewhere.
To follow it, we'll try.

Child: They made their preparations
And set out in their quest,
Following the star at night time,
By day time taking rest.

Chorus: Mile after mile they journeyed on
While overhead the bright star shone.

Children sing: 'Wise Men seeking Jesus'
'Melchior and Balthazar' (*Carol, Gaily Carol*)

Child: At last they came to Bethlehem.
The star stopped moving there,
It hung above a cattle shed,
A stable cold and bare.

We Kings

Child: The wise men found the baby
And knew he was a King.
we Each knelt beside the manger
To give his offering.

ow.

Children sing: 'Now we've Christmas' (*Christmas Things to Sing*, Arnolds)

All children: And now we all keep Christmas
The birthday of this boy,
Who brought to earth great love and peace
And everlasting joy.

All sing: 'In the bleak mid-winter'.

LISTEN, LISTEN

Words: Mrs C. Dixon

Melody: Mrs C. Dixon
Harmony: Mr R. Leach

List—en, list—en, For We have a sto—ry to tell

It's a sto—ry of joy, It's a sto—ry of love, It's a

sto—ry of peace a—mong men. It tells of a

hap—pen—ing Long time a—go, When a ba—by was born to a

girl. And the joy and the love Which we all feel just now Is be-cause of the hap-pen-ing then.

Listen, Listen,
For we have a story to tell
It is a story of joy,
It's a story of love,
It's a story of peace among men.
It tells of a happening
Long time ago,
When a baby was born to a girl.
And the joy and the love
Which we all feel just now
Is because of the happening then.

Listen, Listen,
For we want all people to know
That the baby brought joy
That the baby brought love
That the baby brought peace among men.
Today we are carolling
With all our hearts
And the carol rings out sweet and clear
For the baby was Jesus whose love is the same
Even now as it was even then.

Listen, Listen,
For we have something to say.
We all can know joy
And we all can know love
And we all can know peace among men.
Today we can know it,
Tomorrow the same
If we let Christmas stay in our hearts
For that baby born on a night long ago
Brings us love as He did even then.

GIFTS FOR A KING

A play with mime for younger children, by Christine Mahoney

(This play was written to be performed in church. The children who do not have speaking parts form a choir at one side of the church. The Sanctuary acts as the stable.)

Narrator 1: A long time ago and far away
A little child was born,
No room, no bed, just his mother's arms
And straw to keep him warm.
And yet this child was God's own Son,
So helpless yet so great,
His birth foretold by a shining star
After many centuries' wait.

[*Gabriel appears at lectern. Mary looks frightened and kneels.*]

Gabriel: Peace be with you. Do not be afraid. I come from the Lord to tell you that you are to have a baby boy. He will be called Jesus and he is the Son of God.

Mary: May it be as God wishes.

[*Gabriel and Mary remain still as two verses of 'The Angel Gabriel from heaven came' are sung by the children.*]

Narrator 2: The seasons changed, the year drew on
And Mary thought and prayed
She was the wife of Joseph now (*Enter Joseph*)
A carpenter by trade.

This was the age of Roman rule,
Orders went out for the men
To return to the town of their family line,
For Joseph, Bethlehem.

[*Joseph mimes working: stops and pulls out scroll. Reads it then goes to Mary.*]

26

Joseph: There is a census and we must go to Bethlehem. Do not worry. I will look after you. [*Helps Mary with cloak.*]

[*Mary and Joseph process down centre aisle and round back of church to 'Bethlehem', (front left) while children sing 'Little Donkey'. Finish in front of choir.*] Brownies   Little Donkey.

Narrator 3: A long hard journey they had had
To that poor and sleepy town,
But they reached it at last on a wintry day
As the sun was going down.

It grew dark and cold and the stars came out
Yet they found no place to stay;
People were very sorry, but no,
The town had been full for days.

No 24   V 1, 3, 4

[*As one verse of 'O Little Town of Bethlehem' is played by solo recorder, Mary and Joseph mime knocking on doors in front of choir. Children mime 'no room' by shaking their heads. Mary and Joseph reach Innkeeper and his wife.*]

Joseph: We have been travelling for days and are tired and cold. My wife is to have a baby very soon. Have you any room at all?

Innkeeper: I am sorry, sir. All our rooms are taken.

Innkeeper's wife: We cannot turn them away. Come with me.

[*Innkeeper's wife leads Mary and Joseph to 'stable' while Narrator 4 is speaking. Innkeeper and wife then take up position slightly behind and to the left of Holy Couple.*]

Narrator 4: At the Inn the landlord and his wife
Took pity on Mary's plight,
For, tired and worn, she now was sure
The babe would be born that night.

They showed them the stable, old but dry
Warmed by the breath of ox and ass
And there in that place so plain and bare
The Angel's prophecy came to pass.

[*Carol: Two verses of 'Once in Royal David's City' during which Angels (one of whom hands baby to Mary) take up position behind Mary and Joseph.*]

27   No 18 V 1, 3.

Narrator 5: Out in the fields the Shepherds heard
The Angels sing for joy.
And when their fear was calmed, they came
With gifts for the baby boy.

A sheepskin soft and snug to keep
The baby Jesus warm,
And a shepherd's crook for the days to come
For this was our Saviour born.

[Carol: 'While Shepherds Watched Their Flocks by Night'. No 15
Everyone sings all verses. Shepherds (from right of church)
act out carol verse by verse with Angel Gabriel coming down
to guide them, and finish in tableau, having offered gifts to
baby Jesus. Mary wraps baby in the sheepskin and Joseph
takes the crook.]

[During the next narration Three Kings appear from behind
altar (or side if Church layout does not permit) and process
round in front of stable scene, to take up position at far right.
We did not have them presenting their gifts, merely holding
them up and bowing to the baby, having explained to the children that the kings took two years to find Jesus.]

Narrator 6: A star shone over Bethlehem.
And over all the earth;
Three kings in the East set out to find   *Enter Kings*
The place of the new king's birth.

They carried gifts of gold and myrrh
And precious frankincense,
Royal gifts for the Prince of Peace
Asleep in innocence.

[Carol: two verses of 'Away in a Manger'] No 10.

Narrator 7: What of our gifts? What can we bring?
We have no lambs, no gold.
But we can bring the infant prince
Things that you cannot hold.

A will to work, a heart to love,
Two hands to serve and pray,
We bring you these, dear Lord and King,
We bring you these today.

Rebecca

[*All children, including those in the choir and their teachers, come to front of church and kneel down around the crib. All sing last verse of 'In the Bleak Midwinter'.*]

What can I give him
Poor as I am?
If I were a shepherd
I would bring a lamb;
If I were a wise man
I would do my part;
Yet what I can I gave him —
Give my heart.

1985

No 1. O Come all Ye Faithful.

LITTLE STAR'S BIG NIGHT OUT

A puppet play by
Peter Charlton

Although written for and originally performed by puppets, both this play and the one which follows can be easily adapted for human actors. Playing time is under five minutes, as they were designed to be part of a Family Service. It is helpful if the appropriate Gospel reading immediately precedes the play.

Gospel: St Matthew 2. 1-23

[*There is a background of twinkling stars.*]

Narrator: Once upon a time, many years ago, in the sky there was a star. In fact there were many stars, thousands and thousands of them, twinkling brightly every night. But this story is about just one of them. He wasn't a very big star and I'm sorry to say he didn't twinkle very brightly at all. In fact, he hardly had the energy to glimmer.

[*The Star limps on dejectedly.*]

Star: Oh, I'm fed up. Look at them, all my sisters and brothers and cousins and aunts and uncles — all glittering away up there, bright as ... as ... er — stars. And look at me — yes, I know what you're thinking. You're thinking I'm dull, aren't you? Well, you're right, I am. The dullest star in the Heavens, that's me. If anyone ever invents the Guinness Book of Records, I'll be in it — the dullest star in the universe. Ooh, I'm fed up. Well, nothing every happens up here. You're expected to get up there night after night and twinkle. And what for, eh? I'll tell you what for — nothing, that's what for! Ooh, I'm fed up.

[*He goes into the corner and sulks. Whilst he's in the middle of his sulk, an Angel enters.*]

Angel: Little star?

Star: Go away.

Angel: No, little star, I won't go away. Listen to me, I have an important job for you to do.

Star: Go away, I'm too dull to be spoken to by anyone. I'm too dull to twinkle even on a foggy night. No-one ever wants to talk to me or ask me to do any ... did you say, Important Job?

Angel: Yes, I did. God has given you an important job which must be done tonight.

Star: Why me? There are millions of brighter and better stars around up here. Why pick on me?

Angel: Perhaps, little star, it's because, although you think you're small and dull, he knows that you are capable of shining brighter and better than any star in the Heavens. And that is what you must do tonight.

Star: Ooer.

Angel: This is what you must do. Rise from here, high into the sky, and shine so brightly that all the people on earth will see you and wonder. Move through the skies across the world until you come to the town of Bethlehem. There you will see a stable, in the stable a manger, and in the manger – a baby.

Star: Ah, I love babies.

Angel: This is a very special baby, the most special baby that ever has been born and ever will be born. This baby is the Christ, the Son of our Lord God. And you must tell all men on earth that tonight God's son is born to save mankind.

Star: Cor, that's a big job for a little star.

Angel: You're not a little star, though – you're the biggest, the brightest and the best. You will shine so brightly tonight that mankind will never forget you, wise men will follow you, people will write songs about you. Go and shine for Jesus Christ!

[*The Angel exits.*]

31

Star: Cor! Can I do it? A few exercises and we'll see. [*He attempts a few press-ups, etc.*] Here goes. One, two, three — [*Leaps up into the air and immediately falls down again. Tries another time — no success again.*] I think I need some help. Will you all help me? If you believe I can do it, I will believe I can do it. As they say up here, faith can make stars shine. Ready — go! [*He falters a bit, then slowly begins to rise.*] It's working, I'm shining, I'm twinkling, I'm positively radiating! [*He moves across the stage.*] Hey, you three — follow me! Ah, there's the town of Bethlehem — and there's the stable and .... yes, there's the Baby. All right, you people, start writing the songs — Christ is born! [*He continues shouting praises. We hear the music of the 'We Three Kings' chorus playing:*

'Star of Wonder, Star of Night,
Star of royal beauty bright ....']

THE CHRISTMAS MUMMERS

A puppet play for a Christmas gift-day service, by Peter Charlton

The author writes: I used the 'Mummers' style for several reasons. We are severely restricted for space in our church/hall and the play can be done almost without movement. No part is particularly big and the doggerel verse is easy to learn; also it needs to be declaimed more than acted, which children find reasonably easy to do. I cast the play from our youth groups as well as from the Sunday school, thus representing the entire age-group of our church's young people. I've listed the hymns we used, though of course other people may prefer alternatives.

Hymn: 'He gave me eyes so I could see'

> [*The Mummers enter during the last verse of the hymn and line up in front of the altar. The mumming style is that the characters step forward when it is their turn to speak and step back into line at the end of their particular scene.*]

Father Christmas: In come I, old Father Christmas
Whether I'm early or not,
I hope old Father Christmas
Will never be forgot.

I open the door, I enter in,
I hope God's favour we shall win.
You'll hear us sing, you'll hear us play,
You'll see my merry lads act today.

[*God and Angel Gabriel step forward.*]

The one who wears the golden crown
Is the Lord God of high renown.
The other dressed in white, some swell!
That is Archangel Gabriel. [*He steps back.*]

God: Gabriel, angel chief in heaven,
What gift shall unto earth be given?

Gabriel: If you give them what they deserve
Then fire and flood and fear will serve.

God: No, No, I wish to show them all
My love is theirs whate'er befall.
I know - my only son I'll send
To prove that my love has no end.

Gabriel: This, surely, Lord of land and sea,
Is the greatest gift there'll ever be!

Congregation sing: 'God is love.'

Father Christmas: The next to walk into our play
Is man - a common man, you'd say.
He's Joseph, carpenter by trade.
On him a special task's been laid.

Joseph: From Nazareth I've crossed this nation
Just to be listed for taxation.
I must be daft to take such trouble
So those Romans can tax me double.

[*Mary steps forward.*]

But it's Mary, my wife, I worry for,
Her baby's due at any hour.
An angel told me in a vision
This child is Christ, the King of Heaven.

Mary: Joseph dear, I cannot stand,
I think my time is near at hand.
Is there no place in this whole town
That we may find to lay me down?

Joseph: I've tried each inn along the way
But still can't find a place to stay.
The wind's been blowing fit to freeze.
Innkeeper, won't you help us, please?

Choir sing: 'Standing in the rain' by Sydney Carter

Innkeeper: I cannot leave them on the streets
On such a freezing night.
Her baby must be almost due,
I'll have to heed their plight.
Come, sir, come, madam, follow me,
It's only an old stable,
But there you both may spend the night
As well as you are able.

[*They move back to where a stool and crib have been brought in.*]

Father Christmas: Upon a hillside, close at hand,
Three shepherds tended sheep.
Their flocks were settled for the night,
The men were near asleep.
Just then there came a blinding flash
That caused them much affright,
And there before them on that hill
Was an angel, shining bright.

Gabriel: Fear not but rise, to Bethlehem go,
As fast as you are able.
There you will find the King of Kings
Born lowly in a stable.

1st Shepherd: Let's run!

2nd Shepherd: No, wait, a king he said.
Some gifts we'll have to take.

3rd Shepherd: I'll take a lamb, babies like lambs.
A fine present that will make.

1st Shepherd: I'll take my flute - one day perhaps
He'll want to learn to play.

2nd Shepherd: I'll take my fiddle and perhaps
A tune for his birthday.

[*The three Shepherds play the tune of the Spanish carol* 'What shall I give to the child in the manger?']

[*Congregation sing to the carol.* Note: We used recorder — for flute — violin and tambourine, but other instruments may be substituted as available. *At the end of the carol, the Shepherds turn to the crib and kneel.*]

1st Shepherd: O blessed babe of Bethlehem,
Accept these gifts we bring.

2nd Shepherd: Now everyone, come bring your gifts
To Jesus Christ, our King.

[*Piano/organ plays incidental music while the congregation bring up their gifts to the altar. The Mummers assist in the acceptance of gifts.*]

Mary: For all your gifts we thank you now,
But remember, great and small,
That this small child in manger laid
Is the greatest gift of all.

Congregation sing: 'Away in a Manger' *while Mummers process out.*

The service may end here, with the priest giving the Blessing. We continued with an abbreviated Communion, concluding with 'Hark, the glad sound'.

Costume for the Mummers can be almost anything you wish. God needs to be dressed in something extra grand, plus a golden crown. Some mummers' groups make costumes from newspapers, in strips — books on folk costumes may have pictures that would help. The hymn 'He gave me eyes' is from *Someone's Singing, Lord* and the Spanish carol from *Carol, Gaily Carol,* both published by A & C Black.

THE COMING OF THE LIGHT

Deaconess Jean Naylor devised this piece of dance and drama for a Christingle service

The very popular Christingle services sponsored by the Church of England Children's Society lend themselves to an exploration of the theme of Light, and it was with this in mind that Deaconess Jean Naylor devised a piece of dance and drama for a group of 7s to 9s to enact during the service. She writes: 'We put Roman soldiers, dancers, water-carriers and other crowd parts into the village scene. Two seven-year-olds danced the Annunciation scene beautifully. We used music from the record *Medieval and Early Renaissance Music* by Musica Antiqua, but other music could be adapted. The service raised £100 for the Children's Society'.

Narrator: In the beginning God created Light, but man seemed to prefer darkness rather than light, and so found himself wandering in the darkness. But light was stronger than darkness, and a few people continued to hope for him who was to be the Lord of Light. Malachi, one who looked for the light, came among the people.

[*Music for temple scene as Malachi enters. Fades quietly when he speaks, then comes up higher.*]

Malachi: This is what the Lord says: 'See, the Lord you are waiting for will come to his temple. He will make you holy, and you will be more precious than gold or silver. Then what you offer will be really valuable. You will give your whole heart and will be welcomed by God'.

Narrator: And so the years passed, with just a small group of people still waiting in hope. One of the people was a young village girl named Mary, who was chosen to carry the light into the world.

[*Music .... dance out the Annunciation story with Mary and Gabriel.*]

Narrator: So Jesus, the light of the world, was born and spread the light to all men, bringing them out of darkness to his marvellous light.

[*Music with people moving about a village ... music fades as man rushes in.*]

1st Man [*excitedly*]: I can see ... look, I can see you .... the prophet from Nazareth has opened my eyes. [*He stops and looks at a woman beside him.*] Why, Ruth, you are not crippled any more ... what has happened?

1st Woman: That same Jesus has healed me and I can stand up and face the light.

[*After chattering and excitement, rich man enters giving money.*]

2nd Woman: Isaac, what ails you? Why do you give us money?

Isaac: Jesus has opened my eyes to see what is the real treasure in the world.

[*Music .... all go off rejoicing.*]

Narrator: And so Jesus brought sight to the blind, healing to the sick and new life to all men. He who is the Light of the world gives light to all men.

[*Music .... enter child carrying candle .... places it on altar.*]

Child: We believe in God, the Father, maker of all things. We believe in Jesus Christ, his Son, our Lord. He is the light of the world leading us to the glory of God. We believe in the Holy Spirit, filling our hearts and minds with light, so that we can love and believe in light. Then let us go in the light of God's love.

[*All light Christingles and process out.*]

QUEST FOR A KING

A nativity play by Tom H. Jones written for junior children

Cast:

First Shepherd
Second Shepherd
Third Shepherd
Fourth Shepherd
Melchior
Caspar
Balthazar
Gabriel
Attendant Angels
Dancing Girls

Herod
Roman Governor
Witch
Magician
Magician's Servants
Palace Guards
Guard Commander
Innkeeper
Joseph
Mary
Children in National Costume
Small choir

ACT ONE: A hill outside Bethlehem

Carol: 'In the Bleak Midwinter'

[*A shepherd enters bearing skins of wine and some bread.*]

1st Shepherd: Where have you been? We are dying of hunger waiting for you to bring us our supper. This cold night air bites into my bones, without a drop of wine in my stomach to keep it out.

2nd Shepherd: You've been sitting in the Inn, haven't you? I'll bet you've been roasting yourself over a big log fire while we have been shivering here waiting for our bread and wine.

3rd Shepherd: I'm sorry, but I couldn't help it. Bethlehem is crammed with people this evening. I've never seen so many. Everybody is trying to buy bread and wine and there are queues of people everywhere. I had to wait ages for these, and pay twice the normal price.

39

1st Shepherd: Ah, of course. I should have remembered. The census is on.

2nd Shepherd: The what is on?

1st Shepherd: The census. I'll explain. All people who were born in Bethlehem, no matter where they now live, must put their name on the great book and get counted — that's what a census is.

3rd Shepherd: And that reminds me — we haven't done it yet. They'll punish those who forget.

2nd Shepherd: Never mind. There's plenty of time. We'll do it tomorrow. Oh, I've just thought, we can't write. What will we do?

1st Shepherd: We'll make our marks, of course, the same as a lot of others. I've heard that the mighty Herod himself can't write his own name. So we'll be in good company.

Melchior [*voice heard off stage*]: Hello there!

2nd Shepherd: What's that? [*jumps to his feet and looks through auditorium*] I think I can see three men coming up the hill.

[*The Three Kings enter through auditorium.*]

Melchior: Good evening, friends. May we share your fire for a while? We have journeyed many miles.

[*The shepherds talk together.*]

1st Shepherd: Who are you? We are only poor shepherds, as you can see. We haven't anything you can steal.

Caspar: Bless you, friends. We are not robbers. All we ask is a share of your fire and a rest for our weary bodies.

3rd Shepherd: Well, all right. Sit here. But you can't blame us for being careful. Only last week we had three lambs stolen by robbers.

[*All settle around the fire.*]

1st Shepherd: Have you journeyed far? You don't live in these parts. Your dress is most odd, if you'll pardon my saying so.

Balthazar [*laughing*]: You are right, friend. We have come from far away in the East on a journey that has taken us through many strange lands.

Melchior: But now we think we are nearing the end of our quest. In fact, I think that you could possibly help us.

Balthazar: Yes, I am sure you could. We are looking for the new King of the Jews.

2nd Shepherd: I expect you mean King Herod. He lives miles away in the big palace. Are you friends of his?

Melchior: No, we have never set eyes on him before. In fact, I am surprised you know his name because no one has ever met him before, for tonight he will be born.

[*The shepherds laugh.*]

1st Shepherd: That's a good one. Born tonight indeed. Old Herod's got a beard to his feet. He carries on like a naughty child sometimes, I grant you, but born tonight, oh dear me no. You have made a mistake, sir.

Caspar [*gets to his feet*]: But this can't be true. We have read in the stars that a young child, who will be King of the Jews, will be born tonight in Bethlehem.

Melchior [*gets out a scroll*]: Look, I have made hundreds of calculations. I have checked and cross-checked every detail, I can't be wrong.

Balthazar: And see, there in the sky — that magnificent star. We have followed it across deserts and rivers and now it hovers over this place. Beneath that star, tonight, the King will be born.

1st Shepherd: Steady on, sirs. There is no need to get excited. You've been told the old tale about a brave new king who will be born to save us poor people. My mother used to tell me that story.

2nd Shepherd: My mother, too. Any king would be better than Herod. He's mean and cruel and bad tempered and, and — oh, words fail me.

Melchior: No, friends, we have not heard that tale you tell of. We have read it in the stars and tonight we are convinced he WILL be born.

3rd Shepherd: Well, if you must go to Herod's palace, be careful what you say. If this baby that you speak of is not there, then Herod will not rest until he finds him, and that will be the end of your baby king.

Caspar: Perhaps we had better make our way to the palace. Thank you for the rest, good shepherds. Now if you will point the way, we will leave you.

[*The shepherds show the Kings the way to the Palace.*]

1st Shepherd: Follow this path as far it goes.

2nd Shepherd: When you come to the city, you will see the palace in the distance — you can't miss it.

All: Goodbye, goodbye.

[*Kings exit through auditorium.*]

3rd Shepherd [*shouts after the Kings*]: Remember what we said about Herod.

[*The shepherds re-kindle the fire and prepare for the night.*]

2nd Shepherd [*to 1st Shepherd*]: It's your turn to guard the flocks tonight. Do try to stay awake.

3rd Shepherd: The last time you stood guard, a wolf took two lambs.

1st Shepherd: All right — you needn't rub it in. I'll take care.

[*Lights dim. Two shepherds wrap their cloaks around themselves and settle by the fire. 1st Shepherd sits apart holding crook in hand.*]

[*The Archangel Gabriel, leading small angels, enters through auditorium. They all bear lanterns to light their way.*]

Choir sings: 'The Angel Gabriel' (*The Galliard Book of Carols*)

Gabriel: Be not afraid. [*There is no movement from the shepherds.*]

[*Gabriel clears his throat.*]

Gabriel [*much louder*]: Be not afraid.

[*The shepherds instantly leap to their feet and cower together.*]

Gabriel: Be not afraid.

1st Shepherd: Be off with you. Frightening us like that. Go on, go away, and take your children with you. [*He threatens Gabriel. Gabriel raises his hand and the shepherds remain motionless.*]

Gabriel: Be not afraid. I bring you good tidings and news of great joy which the whole people will share. Today, in David's town, there has been born for you a Saviour who is Christ the Lord. Know by this token — you will find the babe in swaddling clothes lying in a manger.

Angels: Glory to God in the highest and on earth peace to men of goodwill.

Gabriel: Now, be at peace, good shepherds. Go and do God's will.

[*Exit Gabriel and Angels. The shepherds remain still for a second, then rub their eyes.*]

2nd Shepherd: It must be a dream. Here, pinch me to see if I'm awake.

[*3rd Shepherd pinches him.*]

2nd Shepherd: Ouch! This is no dream.

1st Shepherd: Brothers, we have been honoured by God. Those three Kings from the east were right. Tonight our Lord will be born. Come, let us hurry to Bethlehem or we'll be too late.

Carol: 'Go, tell it on the mountain' (*Carol, Gaily Carol*)

[*All hurry off.*]

ACT TWO: Herod's Palace

[*Slave girls perform dance for Herod, who sits moping on his throne.*]

Herod: Stop! Stop! Get out, all of you. I am in no mood for dancing.

[*Dancing girls run off in terror. Herod slumps miserably on his throne.*]

Herod: I cannot get this new King out of my mind. Who is he? And, more important - where is he? I must find him and destroy him before he destroys me.

Roman Governor: I, too, have heard of this so-called King. The city is buzzing with rumours. Know this, Herod: if the people follow him, it will go bad for you. And do not expect help from Rome. We will have dealings with the King of Jews *whoever* he may be.

Herod: Whoever he may be? I am King of the Jews and I will hunt this impostor down. He will be destroyed, do you hear? Destroyed.

Roman Governor: But first, Herod, you must find him. Have your guards hunted him down yet?

Herod: I have offered a fortune in gold to anyone who can lead me to this infant Messiah. Many have come forward, but none have succeeded. Even now I have two people waiting to claim the reward. [*To his Guard*] .... Bring in the witch.

[*Guard goes off.*]

Herod [*to Roman*]: We will hear them together. Perhaps this time I will be lucky.

[*The Witch enters, carrying a crystal ball.*]

Guard: Here is the witch, my Lord. She claims to see all in her magic crystal.

Herod: I hope she sees her own death in it if she thinks she can trick me out of my gold. [*To witch*] What do you see, hag?

Witch: I have seen many wonderful things, O Herod, in this magic crystal. And for the reward I will find the infant King.

Herod: That is what they have all said. Give me a sign. Show me some of your magic powers.

Roman: Yes, work some magic for us. Make the sun stop shining or the world stand still.

Witch: I weave no magic spell, Lord, I see only into the future. [*Looks into her crystal*] Herod, your name will be remembered a thousand years from now. When all others here today have long been forgotten, your name will still spring to people's lips. You will be written about in plays and books and songs and never will the name of Herod be forgotten.

Herod: Very flattering indeed, old woman, but I am not offering a King's ransom to have *my* fortune told.

Roman: Come, woman, what about this King?

Witch [*gazes into the crystal*]: I see a poor inn nearby. A carpenter and his wife are there. A shepherd enters now and kneels beside the manger. Wait, it is clearer now — yes, I have it — a stable near here and in it a baby.

Herod: Stop, stop, enough of that. Guards, take the old fool away and burn her. A stable, indeed.

Roman: Whoever heard of a King born in a stable! She must think we are mad. Off with her.
[*They reseat themselves, laughing heartily.*]

Herod: Bring in the next one. We may as well hear the last of the fortune hunters.
[*Enter the Magician and his servants, carrying books of magic, wands and other magical impedimenta.*]

Magician [*bows to Herod*]: Your Majesty, I have great powers and I am sure that with my magic I will divine the secret of where this rival King of the Jews will be found.

Herod: If you do this, you will be well rewarded. But do not try to fool me, I warn you. All others I have consulted have failed and my patience is at an end.

Roman: Let us see some of your magic powers, or perhaps, like the others, your magic works only when you are alone.

Magician: Gaze on this, O King, and see if my powers are not great!
[*He calls the servant carrying a tray. On the tray are some nails and a metal bar. Concealed in the Magician's pocket is a powerful magnet.*]

You see this piece of metal ...

[*Shows it to the King and Guards.*]

I wish your Majesty to pick up these nails using only this. You must not touch them with your hands.

[*The King tries but fails.*]

Herod: I cannot get a grip of them. [*Throws down the metal*] It is impossible, I say.

Magician: With my magic, O King, everything is possible. Now watch.

[*He has substituted the piece of metal for a magnet whilst talking. He waves a wand over the magnet and chants magic incantations.*]

By the magic in this arm of mine, come to me, nails, I am your master.

[*The nails are attracted by the magnet and he holds them aloft.*]

[*The Guards and courtiers shrink back in fright.*]

Roman: Keep back - he is indeed a powerful magician. Look ... [*points to magnet*], his power is tremendous.

Herod: Your power is indeed great, Magician. Now tell me, where is he that is to be King of the Jews?

Magician: Boy, bring the book. [*He consults his astrological book*] Now let me see, ah yes - a thousand miles from here, deep in a cave a little babe is lying. He is guarded by a monstrous dragon.

Herod: Where is this cave? Take my guards to it.

Magician: Do not fear, your Majesty, no mortal can approach this cave. Only I can destroy him with my magic. But first, your Majesty ...

[*Motions that he wants the gold.*]

Herod: Pay him the money. But mark my words, Magician, if this King is found to live, *you* will lose your life. Now go.

[*Exit Magician with his gold.*]

Roman: I fear, Herod, that you are still no nearer to finding this King.

Herod: Is there no peace for me? I cannot rest until I hear that is he dead.

[*Guard enters and bows.*]

Guard: Your Majesty, three royal men are at the gates of the Palace asking for an infant King of the Jews.

Herod [*leaps to his feet*]: What is that you say? Show them in immediately.

Carol: 'We Three Kings'

[*Kings enter through auditorium during singing.*]

Melchior: Greetings, your Majesty. We have travelled far to witness the birth of your baby son – the new King of the Jews.

Balthazar: We have brought gifts and with your Majesty's permission we will present them to the infant King.

Herod: How very interesting, gentlemen. But at the moment I am the only King of the Jews here. There is no infant King.

Roman: But if what you say is true, we would be overjoyed and we would dearly love to see this infant.

Herod: Yes, tell me. Where will he be born?

Caspar: We thought we would find him here, your Majesty, but obviously we are wrong. We will have to journey on seeking him once more.

Herod: But let me help. Allow me to accompany you on your journey, so that I may act as your guide through Jerusalem. I, too, have a small gift I would like to give him on his birthday. [*He smiles at the guards as he handles the hilt of his sword.*]

Caspar: I think that would be .....

Melchior [*cuts Caspar short*]: Thank you, King Herod, but as the baby is not here, we will have to return to our country to consult our books again. Perhaps we will meet again when we have further news.

Herod: But what was your information? You *must* have had information.

Balthazar: We have divined that a Royal King would be born tonight. A Messiah, a leader of men, the greatest King the Jews would ever see.

Melchior: Yes, but obviously, we were wrong. So now, Herod, we will bid you goodbye and be on our way.

[*Exit Kings.*]

Roman: Tonight, they said. Did you hear that, Herod? I feel those men knew more than they were prepared to tell us. You must follow them. To the ends of the earth, if needs be.

Herod: Guards, guards.

[*Royal guards come in and assemble before Herod.*]

Follow those men. They are telling lies. They *know* where this child is to be born. Do not let them out of your sight or else you will regret this day. When you discover the place, slay the Kings and bring the babe to me. Now go.

Guard Commander [*salutes with sword*]: It shall be done, your Majesty. Follow me, guards — at the double.

ACT THREE - Outside the Inn
[*The shepherds enter and stand outside the inn door.*]

1st Shepherd: The Angels *did* say that the infant would be born in a manger.

2nd Shepherd: Yes, and we have already looked in at least ten mangers and all we have seen is hay.

3rd Shepherd: Anyway, let us try here. As there are so many people here, perhaps someone is sleeping in the inn stables.

[*They knock on the door.*]

Innkeeper: It is no use your coming here. I am absolutely full up. I've even got people sleeping in the stable. I've never known anything like it.

1st Shepherd [*excitedly*]: We don't want a room, thank you. Could you tell us, please, are the couple who are staying in the stable expecting a child?

Innkeeper: As a matter of fact, they are. Strange you should ask. There are two people from Nazareth here. They are up for the census. Joseph something or other his name is, and his wife Mary. His family lived here in Bethlehem at one time.

2nd Shepherd: Thank you, Innkeeper. [*To other shepherds*] This is the place. It must be. Let's go in and look.

Innkeeper: Hold on there. Where do you think you are going?

3rd Shepherd: To see the baby, of course.

Innkeeper: Oh, are you indeed? Well, I'll see if all's well first. You can wait out here.

[*Innkeeper goes into the inn. The shepherds sit around the stable door.*]

Choir sings: 'Mary had a baby' (*Carol, Gaily Carol*)

Melchior [*appears through auditorium*]: Hello there!

3rd Shepherd: Who's this? He looks like an official. Come on, you two, let's run for it, he probably wants to know why we haven't signed the census.

Melchior: Wait, friends. I see you have found the place before me. I am not too late, am I? What is the baby like?

1st Shepherd: You gave us a fright. We thought you were one of Herod's men.

2nd Shepherd: You are not too late, sir. We have not yet seen the child.

Melchior: Oh. Good. Then I am in time. This star has led me well.

[*Points to star above the stable.*]

3rd Shepherd: Shh. Quiet, sir. Please do not speak so loudly. Someone is sure to hear us. Herod has spies everywhere. He, and only he, must be thought of as King of the Jews. [*Baby cries*] That is, until now.

[*They all crowd around the door all talking together and asking if anything can be seen.*]

1st Shepherd: Shh. Shh. Quiet everyone. You'll frighten the baby.

Carol: 'Come, see this little stranger' (*Carol, Gaily Carol*)

Innkeeper [*comes out*]: It's a boy, a beautiful baby boy. They are going to call him Jesus. Now wait here, please, and do calm yourselves and keep quiet.

[*The other two Wise Men appear through auditorium.*]

Caspar: This must be the place, Balthazar. Look, there is the star. Well, that inn isn't my idea of a King's birthplace. But still, that is where the infant King will be.

Balthazar: I wonder what happened to Melchior. After leaving Herod's palace he went off at a terrific pace on his camel — and he knew my camel had gone lame. I do think he could have waited.

Caspar: Look, there he is, standing there with those men. Hey! Melchior, Melchior.

Melchior: Come along, Caspar. I thought you and Balthazar had lost the way. This is the place, our search is over. Good people [*addresses shepherds*] I have wonderful news for you. The child who has just been born is the Messiah for whom we have long been searching. He is the Son of God, prophesied in our Holy Book.

2nd Shepherd: We know. After you left us we were visited by Angels who told us the good news.

3rd Shepherd: We left straightaway and hurried to be present at his birth.

[*Palace guards appear in auditorium — they look intently at audience as they approach the stage.*]

Caspar: Look, Balthazar, there are those men who have been following us. I am sure Herod has sent them to find the baby and destroy him.

Balthazar: We must hide or they will realise the baby is here. Quickly, look around for a hiding place.

2nd Shepherd: Here, I know. Off with your crowns quickly and slip our cloaks over you.

[*They don the cloaks and all huddle outside the inn.*]

3rd Shepherd: We'll pretend we are all shepherds waiting for the inn to open.

Guard Commander: You, there, have you seen three men passing this way? They were richly dressed with crowns on their heads. Speak up quickly.

1st Shepherd: No, sir. We are poor shepherds and we haven't seen a soul! We are waiting here to buy wine and bread, but everything is so scarce and very, very, expensive.

Commander: Well, keep your eyes open and get off the streets before curfew or you'll end up in prison. [*They turn to go.*]

3rd Shepherd: Wait, sir, I did see someone. Did those men look like foreigners and have camels with them?

Commander: Yes. Speak up, man, have you seen them?

2nd Shepherd: Yes, I did, not half an hour ago. If you go up here to the crossroads and take the road to Jerusalem you will catch them — they can't have gone far.

Commander: Quickly, men follow me, on the double now.

[*Exit at the trot. All laugh heartily.*]

Melchior: That's got rid of them. Thank you, good shepherds, you have done well this night and your reward will be great.

Innkeeper: You can all see the baby now, his father is bringing him out.

[*Enter Joseph and Mary with Baby in cradle.*]

Joseph: We have been expecting you. Here is the child you have journeyed far to see.

Carol: 'See him a-laying in a bed of straw' (*Merrily to Bethlehem,* A&C Black)

Melchior [*walks to crib and kneels*]: I give this child gold, to show that amongst all men he will be King.

Caspar: Frankincense is my gift. This will show that he will lead men to worship and pray.

Balthazar: I give myrrh, to show that he will be a great healer of the sick.

[*The shepherds whisper together.*]

2nd Shepherd [*to 1st Shepherd*]: What have you got? Here, take this [*gives crook*].

1st Shepherd: We give this [*presents shepherd's crook*] to show that he will be the Good Shepherd and we his humble flock.

Balthazar [*steps forward to audience*]: The King born tonight shall be King of all, whatever their nationality, colour or creed. I call now the children of the future, of all nations, to worship our infant King.

[*Enter procession of Children of All Nations, preceded by Angels, bearing gifts in rich packages which they place around the tableau.*]

Melchior [*steps forward*]: Tonight we have witnessed the birth of our Lord - Jesus Christ. From now on, every Christmas Day, the whole world will celebrate his birthday with great joy and thanksgiving. But all birthdays sometimes slip our memories, even this one; we may forget the true reason for our celebrations. So let me remind you now and invite you all to his birthday celebrations this year — 19 ....

Carol: 'Gloria, gloria' (*Merrily to Bethlehem*).

THE GUEST

**Isobel Galilee has dramatised
this famous seventeenth century poem
for presentation by juniors
or a mixed-age group of children**

Narrator: Yet if his majesty, our sovereign lord,
Should of his own accord
Friendly himself invite,
And say, I'll be your guest tomorrow night ...

[*Messenger comes up aisle with scroll.*]

How we should stir ourselves, call and command ...

Lord of the Manor: All hands to work! Let no man idle stand!
Set me fine Spanish tables in the Hall,
See they be fitted all ...

[*Tables put up in chancel and aisle.*]

Let there be room to eat,
And order taken that there want no meat ...

[*Chairs put in place - top table first. Mugs, bowls, etc., put on tables. Bread in baskets.*]

See every sconce and candlestick made bright,
That without tapers they may give light ...

[*Candlesticks carried up aisle, rubbed with dusters, put on top table.*]

Look to the presence, are the carpets spread,
The daïs o'er the head?

[*Carpet put in front of top table. Screen moved behind top table and manger put in place behind screen.*]

The cushions on the chairs,
And all the candles lighted on the stairs?

[*Cushions put on chair of top table. Candles lit.*]

Perfume the chambers and in any case
Let each man give attendance in his place.

[*Sprays of rosemary strewn on floor. Servants come from back of church, stand by their chairs. Fanfare as King and attendants come up aisle. Everyone bows and curtsies. Lord of Manor shows him to his seat. King sits, then everyone else. Food shared.*]

Music: 'Deck the hall with boughs of holly'

Narrator: Thus, if the King were coming, would we do,
And 'twere good reason too,
For 'tis a duteous thing
To show all honour to an earthly king;
And after all our travail and our cost,
So he be pleased, to think no labour lost.

[*King rises, bows to Lord of the Manor, exits with attendants left. Fanfare. Everyone bows and curtsies.*]

Narrator: But at the coming of the King of Heaven,
All's set at six and seven.
We wallow in our sin ...

[*Everyone sits down and relaxes, elbows on table and so on — a chance for bad table manners!*]

Christ cannot find a chamber in the Inn.
We entertain him always like a stranger,
and as at first, still lodge him in a manger.

[*Mary and Joseph come up the aisle, mime asking for shelter. Everyone shakes their head or ignores them. Eventually one or two people from the choir lead them behind the screen. Enter angels and shepherd from left, join Mary and Joseph. Re-enter choir members from behind screen; they — or the whole choir — sing, with drama and urgency, first verse of carol. All join in second and third verse.*]

Bring a torch, Jeanette, Isabella,
Bring a torch, to the stable run.
It is Jesus, good folk of the village.
Christ is born and Mary calls us.
Ah! Ah! Beautiful is the Mother,
Ah! Ah! Beautiful is the Son.

'Jeanette' and 'Isabella' jump up from table, pick up candles from top table, and go behind screen.

Cloudless is the sky above us,
Leave your table and quietly come,
It is Jesus, good folk of the village,
Christ is born and Mary calls us.
Ah! Ah! Beautiful is the Mother,
Ah! Ah! Beautiful is the Son.

First the top table, then the screen are cleared away, revealing manger scene. Everyone goes to group round manger.

See who knocks at the door so loudly,
See who knocks, good people, see.
Open please that he may adore him,
Lay his treasure down before him.
Ah! Ah! Beautiful is the Mother,
Ah! Ah! Beautiful is the Son.

*Knocks.
Re-enter king and attendants from left, kneel before manger, present gifts.*

[*To end the play, Mary and Joseph pick up baby and walk smiling down the aisle, followed by rest of cast while more music is played.*]

Notes on 'The Guest'

The poem on which this play is based is to be found in *The Oxford Book of Seventeenth Century Verse* and other anthologies. The author is unknown. I have changed only the spelling, and the word 'däis', which in the original is 'dazie', meaning 'daïs or canopy'. The phrase 'o'er the head' suggests the latter meaning, and we in fact used a screen which both provided a decorative background for the king's chair, and hid the manger from view until the end of the play.

Although the poem is a seventeenth-century one, the details fit a vaguely medieval setting, and the lay-out of a 'top table' across the chancel at right angles to other tables in the aisle is exactly that of a medieval hall, even down to the screen or canopy behind the top table. We found it helped to have the aisle tables lower in height than the top table, so that the chancel could be seen clearly.

This play suits children who are bored with being cast as angels or shepherds, as there is plenty for both boys and girls to do as the servants. All the servants came from the back of the church to perform their tasks and returned there until the entrance of the king. I also used a group of children, mostly from our church choir, to play recorder music and sing as 'medieval minstrels'. Further entertainment could be provided for the king if there are children available who could perform such medieval amusements as juggling or tumbling!

We laid the tables with mugs, tankards, bowls, etc., made only of pewter, wood or pottery, which gave a surprisingly authentic-looking effect. There is no need to lay a place for each person, except on the top table, as jugs and bowls can be passed round. The feast was represented only by rolls of brown bread, and this convention was accepted readily. The 'wallowing in sin' part was a riot at rehearsal but on the day itself the 'sin' was hardly noticeable — so this part needs careful rehearsal.

We borrowed or made costumes for the Lord of the Manor, King and Messenger, and Mary and Joseph wore modified versions of the usual biblical costume so that they would be recognisable. The boy servants were asked to wear a loose-fitting shirt or sweater, belted at the waist, and trousers buckled into boots or 'cross-gartered'. The girls were asked to wear long skirts, and a plain sweater or shawl, with head-scarves tied at the nape of the neck. The results were quite effective and easy for parents to provide.

The French carol 'Bring a Torch' can be found in *Carols of the Nations* compiled by Ruth Heller (Blandford Press) and, under the title 'Run with torches', in *Carol, Gaily Carol* (A & C Black). I used the words from both versions so that I could bring the king back to pay homage. Other carols describing the finding of the baby in the stable could be used.

The Lord of the Manor can, of course, have his words printed for reference, if necessary, on the scroll handed to him by the messenger at the beginning.

THE CAMEL MEN

Luton headmaster Clarence Johnson wrote for his junior children this unusual story of two thieves

This piece could be performed just as speech, perhaps with the 'One voice' part split up between several narrators, or it could be used as the narration to a mime play. In that event the 'action' for the last two verses might be the use of three crosses silhouetted against a suitably lit background, or some other symbolic representation involving lighting.

Speaking parts:
One voice
Two voices in chorus
Herod

Acting parts:
Two thieves
Three kings
Herod
Soldiers, mothers with babies

One voice: 'What seek you, travellers?'

Two voices: 'A star.
To guide us on our way.

One voice: 'You must be weary. Rest.'

Two voices: 'We are.
We rest at break of day.
Most roads we take
but to forsake
This way and that we wend,
Our way unsure
The night obscure
We seek a light that will endure
Until our journey's end.'

One voice: There were two thieves in days of old
Whose guiding star was one of gold.
It lured them on to wealth untold
But never showed them where.

They'd purses filch and homes ransack,
They'd have the shirt right off your back
Would Al-Nashnir and Shakashak —
An avaricious pair!

They travelled on from place to place,
Would rob and swindle for a space,
And then be gone without a trace —
Both melted into air.

And still they followed that same star
Until within a town's bazaar
They met three strangers from afar
And ceased their search right there —

Because before them they could see
Three men of wealth and high degree
Whose riches seemed to them to be
The answer to their prayer.

One voice: 'What seek you, travellers?'

Two voices: 'A king
To worship and obey.'

One voice: 'Gifts we bring
before his throne to lay.

We would behold
The one foretold
Whose star now shines on high.
Its light our guide
As on we ride
And nowhere may we long abide
While it is in the sky.'

One voice: Then Shakashak and Al-Nashnir
Approached the three to volunteer
As camel-drivers for a year
And ride with them.

They hoped a chance would come one day
To steal the strangers' wealth away
Which would be just as soon as they
Devised a stratagem.

For many months they journeyed on,
With chances that were missed and gone,
Until at length they came upon
The town Jerusalem.

They watched King Herod scrutinise
The kings and weigh up their replies,
Blind terror in the shifty eyes
Beneath the diadem.

Then later on a summons came
For both the thieves in Herod's name,
He rounded on them to exclaim:

Herod: 'You go to Bethlehem!'

Herod: 'What seek you, travellers?'.

Two voices: 'That, sire,
      Which gives a fair reward.'

Herod: 'Then do my will.'

Two voices: 'We are for hire.
      Henceforth you are our lord.

      Our masters are
      Led by this star
      To Bethlehem, you say.
      We'll see you hear
      When they are near
      This infant king whom they revere,
      If you're prepared to pay.'

One voice: The thieves, their journey's end in sight
      Rode with their masters through the night,
      The star above still shining bright
      And moving on ahead.

      And so they came to Bethlehem
      And saw the star, a blazing gem,
      Now fixed at last, reveal to them
      A humble cattle-shed.

      Then Al-Nashnir and Shakashak,
      Without dismounting, hurried back
      To Herod, showing him the track
      That to his quarry led.

The crime was his, the children slain
Why feel as theirs another's pain,
Why visit Bethlehem again
To look upon the dead?

The star they'd followed had not lied:
Their lust for gold was gratified.
Why sought they then another guide —
A star whose light was fled?

One voice: 'What seek you, travellers?'

Two voices: 'A star
To guide us on our way.'

One voice: 'You must be weary. Rest.'

Two voices: We are.
We rest at break of day.

Most roads we take
But to forsake
This way and that we wend.
Our way unsure,
The night obscure,
We seek a light that will endure
Until our journey's end.'

One voice: Perhaps they found their star. Who knows?
Perhaps they gave up in despair.
Perhaps they went on to the close
Still searching vainly everywhere.

It could have been they found their star,
The one they'd seen at Bethlehem —
Not shining faintly from afar
But close, its glory clear to them.

There were two thieves on either side
Of Christ on Calvary, and one
Might well have seen before he died
A star all golden like the sun.

'THIS IS YOUR LIFE'

The Rev. R.M. Clarke needed a play to be acted by a class of dyslexic boys - hence this original variant on the Nativity theme, with no ladies present!

Cast:

Boy Jesus
Compere
Teachers and Doctor of the Law
Inn Keeper - Ruben
Shepherds - David and Benjamin
King - Melchior
Simeon (on tape)
Joseph

[*Enter group of Teachers and Doctor of the Law. They sit to one side of stage.*]

Compere: The subject of today's programme at this very moment should be on his way to the Temple to talk with the teachers and a doctor of the Law. I will hide here so that I can catch him as he enters.

[*Jesus enters through door at back and makes towards the stage.*]

Compere: Not so fast! For Jesus, son of Mary, boy from Nazareth, this is your life - so far.

Jesus: What? It can't be! How did you know I was coming here?

Compere: The teachers were amazed at your answers when you came to the Temple yesterday. They suggested we found out more about you. [*Music*] Our story goes back to a time you will not remember, but I expect your mother has told you some of it. We start in a most unlikely place with a most unlikely character.

61

Innkeeper Ruben [*offstage*]: I didn't even have time to clean out the cattle trough.

[*Jesus turns to Compere.*]

Compere: Yes, that's right. Here today from Bethlehem, Ruben, the Innkeeper of the 'The Rising Star', come in, please.

[*Ruben walks on to stage.*]

Compere: What do you remember about that night?

Ruben: There were thousands of people in Bethlehem. We were packed out. Good for trade, you understand, but not so good for the heart. We had been turning people away most of the day. In the late afternoon, as it was getting cold, a young couple arrived, and the woman − Mary, that was her name − looked absolutely exhausted. What could I do? We opened up the stable and put up a couple of lamps, scattered some fresh straw on the floor, but the cattle trough never did get cleaned out.

Compere: I am sure Mary would have made her husband deal with that problem. Thank you, Ruben. [*Ruben sits.*] But that wasn't the end of it for poor old Ruben. Very soon his door was being knocked on again.

David: [*offstage*]: Ruben! Have you seen the baby what the angels were on about?

Compere: I am sure Ruben will remember that voice, and his thumping on the door probably woke you up. Yes, it's Chief Shepherd David and his son Benjamin, here from the hillside above Bethlehem where he still farms today.

[*David and Benjamin walk forward.*]

David: It was a beautiful night, clear and crisp. The star twinkled overhead. The sheep were a bit restless. We were sitting round the fire. Suddenly there was this great flash of light. Angels were all around us.

Benjamin: 'Don't be afraid', they said. 'We bring you good news' − nearly frightened the living daylights out of me − 'news of great joy for all people'. Then it was something about a Saviour in Bethlehem, born in a manger of all places. I suppose it must be this chap here!

Compere: What did you do then?

David: We turned to Bethlehem and looked for the manger the angel had spoken about. Then we found poor old Ruben rushed off his feet — but at last we saw the reason for our search: Mary and Joseph and the Baby. Come to think of it, he *was* crying. But we didn't stay long, we gave a sheepskin rug and then left.

[*David and Benjamin sit.*]

Compere: But that wasn't the only visitor you had to the manger.

Melchior [*offstage*]: No, I had come a lot further. Had it not been for the clouds during that week we would have been earlier.

[*Melchior walks on stage.*]

Compere: Yes, flown in all the way from India: Melchior, one of the wise men who came to see you in the manger and also brought you presents.

Melchior: Yes, we had followed the star from the east. Our journey led us to this part of the world, but in the clouds we lost sight of the star and made the mistake of expecting to find the baby in the king's palace. That cost us time and nearly cost you your life, Jesus. We eventually found you, but failed to report back to Herod as he had asked.

Compere: And it was just as well, for we all know how he slaughtered the innocent children in an attempt to find this king of the Jews. Thank you. [*Melchior sits.*] Some time later, at the time of the purification, your Mother and Father took you up to the Temple to present you to God. There you met a man who has since died, but who recorded this message.

Simeon [*on tape*]: Lord, now I can die content, for I have seen him as you promised I would. I have seen the Saviour you have given to the world. He is the light that will shine upon the nations and he will be the glory of your people Israel.

Compere: Yes, that's right, Simeon — the man who received you at your presentation in the Temple. Back in Nazareth you grew up in the house next to Joseph's workshop. As you grew up you must have spent a great deal of time in the carpenter's shop.

Jesus: Yes, I enjoyed that, helping Joseph. But I enjoyed playing with the other children more. We were so excited about our trip to Jerusalem last week, we seemed to spend so little time with our parents as we travelled for the feast of the Passover.

Joseph [*offstage*]: And you haven't seen much of us for the last three days!

[*Joseph walks on stage.*]

Compere: Yes, returned from the caravan on its way back to Nazareth, here to take you home: your earthly father, Joseph. What has he been like at home?

Joseph: He has been a good boy really, but sometimes he seems so far away — as if he's got something else on his mind. Mind you, we knew that there was something very special about him when the angel appeared to the wife and me. At the moment his mother is frantic with worry. Just you wait till I get you home, my lad!

Jesus: Don't be cross, Father. Didn't you expect to find me in my heavenly Father's House?

[*Joseph puts his arm around Jesus.*]

Compere: So there it is, Ladies and Gentlemen. Jesus of Nazareth, Saviour, Christ the Lord, King of the Jews, Light of the Gentiles: This is your life — so far.

[*Music - cast leave stage and Doctor of the Law and Teachers return.*]

Doctor of the Law: It's no wonder he gave us such answers. I wonder what the rest of his life will be like?

THE LIGHT TO LIGHTEN THE WORLD

Another play for a group of junior boys, by Rev. R.M. Clarke

Cast:

Narrator
Melchior
Caspar
Bathazar
Voice
Crowd 1, 2, 3, 4
Stranger
Herod
Messenger

Narrator: Melchior was a wise man of Arabia who studied the heavens. One day in an old book he found a strange promise made by one of the prophets —

Voice: 'A star shall come from the land of Jacob. A king will rise in Israel.'

Narrator: Long ago in the East people believed that a new star appeared in the sky when great kings were born.

Melchior: I wonder when this great King of Israel will come, bringing peace and goodwill.

Narrator: Caspar and Balthazar were also wise men and each night the three of them watched the sky, hoping to see the star appear. One night they saw what they had been waiting for.

Melchior: The Star — at last.

Caspar: The King of Israel, the Saviour of the World, is born.

Balthazar: Let us go and find him.

Narrator: Anxious to see the Saviour, the three men set out on their g,eat adventure, despite the advice from their friends and relations.

Crowd 1: You're mad. This journey is absurd. You don't even know when the king was born or where he is now. How do you expect to find him?

Crowd 2: If you ask me it's just a wild goose chase.

Caspar: Ah, but we didn't ask you.

Crowd 2: Well, fancy leaving your homes and families.

Crowd 3: Just think of the danger involved.

Crowd 4: And just suppose you don't find him. You'll have had a wasted journey and everyone will laugh at you.

Narrator: But the star which they saw led them on. They believed it would lead them to the king. They made hasty preparations and set off across the burning desert towards the land of Israel.

Caspar: We must follow the star.

Melchior: It is showing us the right road.

Balthazar: It is leading us to the king.

Narrator: At last they reached Israel and made for Jerusalem. As they arrived within the city a terrible thing happened. They lost sight of the star.

Caspar: What shall we do?

Balthazar: Have we been mistaken?

Melchior: How can we get help?

Balthazar: Ask someone — go on, ask someone. Here is someone coming.

Caspar: Where is the King of the Jews who has just been born?

Stranger: What? Who is this King of the Jews? In Jerusalem we only know one king — Herod.

Narrator: When news of the foreign visitors and their mission reached Herod he was not very pleased.

Herod: What do these rumours mean? Another king would make my position difficult. I will ask the doctors of the law what they know about the child and where he is. Then I must get rid of him by one means or another.

Narrator: The doctors pointed to Bethlehem as being the appointed place and Herod sent for the wise men so that they could help him put his plan into practice.

Messenger: Come with me to Herod's Palace. The king wants to speak with you.

Balthazar: Perhaps he knows where the new baby is.

Melchior: That would seem right.

Herod: Welcome to our land and our city. I understand you are searching for the King of the Jews. Well, he is to be found in Bethlehem. When you find him, send word to me so that I may be able to go and worship him.

Balthazar: Thank you — thank you, we'll certainly keep you in touch.

Caspar, Melchior: Yes, many thanks for your help.

Narrator: Feeling they were on the right path and encouraged by the fact that they could see the star again, they set off towards Bethlehem, somewhat amazed at the number of travellers on the road. On approaching the town the star appeared to slow down and came to rest over a humble stable.

Melchior: I wonder where the place is.

Caspar: We do not seem to be the only ones here for the celebrations.

Balthazar: That man I spoke to just then said he was here to pay his taxes — that's nothing to celebrate.

Narrator: The star had definitely stopped, so they squeezed through the door.

Balthazar: There is the baby.

Caspar: This is not what we expected — where is the palace and where are the servants?

Melchior: This child is poor. Is this the one who is sent by God to be the Saviour of the world? [*All three kneel.*]

Narrator: They believed in him and made their offerings — gold, frankincense and myrrh. After some time they departed to tell the world of the boy Jesus, born to be Saviour. But they did not return to Jerusalem as Herod had requested. Instead they chose another route back home. An angel had commanded them not to go to Herod and they obeyed.

Balthazar: What will Herod think?

Caspar: Why can't we tell him first?

Melchior: It is better if we simply obey the angel.

Narrator: And that is just what they did. Herod, meanwhile, was becoming more and more anxious and impatient. He realised that he had been tricked.

Joseph had also been visited by the angel and warned about Herod. He and Mary and the baby escaped quickly to Egypt before the wicked king could carry out his threat to kill Jesus.

Meanwhile, the wise men reached home — their task accomplished. Both to the believers and to the people who doubted the star and foretold disaster they said:

Melchior: He who called us and guided us to him by a star has shown himself as the messenger of God.

Caspar: By accepting us strangers he showed clearly that he came for all people and all races.

Balthazar: He calls you too — believe in him.

Narrator: So the wise men were the first missionaries who brought the Good News to a people in darkness. They spoke of the Divine Light which appeared to them at Bethlehem — Jesus, the Son of God.

THE CHILDREN'S CHRISTMAS

A short play for juniors
by Katherine Musson

Narrator: On a dark cold evening in Bethlehem, some children were playing in the street.

Suzanne: Who'd like to play hopscotch? [*Or another game known to the children which they can actually play during the action.*]

Others: Me! Me!

Joanna: I'll start. [*Children play. Pre-taped sound of crowd begins.*]

Narrator: Crowds of people were gathering, taking part in the Emperor's census, then wearily seeking a room for the night, until all the inns were full.

Suzanne: Your turn, Paul.

Voice [*off*]: Paul!

Paul: Yes?

Voice: Will you fetch me some straw, please?

Paul: What for?

Voice: Some people are staying in our stable tonight. Everywhere else is full up. [*Paul collects straw, runs off with it, returns.*]

Joanna: Come on, let's get on with our game. Your turn, Paul.

Voice: Paul!

Voice: Will you fetch me some water, please, quickly?

Paul: Why?

Voice: The lady is having a baby.

[*Paul takes pitcher of water off.*]

Choir sings: First verse only of 'The Zither Carol' (in *Carols for Choirs, Vol. 1*, Oxford University Press)

Joanna: Let's play again.

Suzanne: Your turn, James ...

Alex: Hey! Look at that star in the sky ...

Poppy: Isn't it bright?

All children: Look!

Suzanne: No, I'm scared ... [*Enter Paul*]

Paul: The boy is born ... Come and see!

Elizabeth: Yes, let's all go. [*Children run off*]

Suzanne: Hey, what about the game?

Joanna: I'm playing. What's so special about a baby, anyway?

[*They continue to play.*]

Narrator: Shepherds were crowding round the inn stable now.
Leaving their sheep to fend for themselves
Out on the cold, deserted hillside.

[*Children return from the stable.*]

Elizabeth: There *is* something strange about this baby. All sorts of people are coming to see him. Even the shepherds have left their sheep.

Paul: I'm going to look again.

Alex: Me too.

Poppy: And me.

[*Children return to stable, leaving Suzanne and Joanna.*]

Choir sings: Second verse only of 'The Zither Carol'.

[*Children re-enter from stable.*]

Joanna: Will no-one finish the game?

Suzanne and others: We will!

[*Sounds of arrival of camels, cries of 'Look at the strangers!' 'Look at their crowns!' 'Hold that camel!' etc.*]

Narrator: Suddenly the silence of the night was broken
As a train of camels clattered into view.
Strange men appeared, bejewelled and crowned.
Laden with gifts, they gathered at the stable door.
Gaping with wonder, the children crept
Hand in hand, to behold the amazing sight
Of foreign princes kneeling and bowing their heads
Before a tiny baby.

[*Children, pointing and holding hands, go to stable, leaving Joanna and Suzanne.*]

Suzanne: Will you come too?

Joanna: I suppose so. No-one wants to play the game any more.

Suzanne: There must be something special about this baby if kings travel all that way to see him.

[*Joanna and Suzanne go to stable.*]

Narrator: And so the children were united
With those throughout the ages
Who have gathered round the crib of the infant Jesus
In joy and love and praise.

Choir sings: Last verse of 'The Zither Carol'.

Notes: The names of those originally taking part are used for the children; the actors' own names can be used and any number of children can take part. If there are plenty available, the play could end with a curtain drawn back to reveal a tableau of the Nativity scene with kings, shepherds and children before the manger.

ONE OF US

A play for juniors
set in a gipsy camp
by Margery Robinson

Cast:

Lee, aged 8	Bridget
Becky, 7	Tim
John	Gipsy Mother
Penny	Gipsy Father
Mark	The cast of the Nativity Play to be mimed

SCENE I

[*A bare stage. Becky and Lee enter from the left. They walk around looking, then stop as Becky begins to cry.*]

Lee: Don't cry, Becky, we'll find them, they can't have gone far.

Becky [*looking on the ground*]: Look, there's the caravan tracks.

Lee: Then they've been moved on, the man from the council said we'd have to go.

Becky: They've left us behind. [*In panic grabs her brother's arm.*] What shall we do?

Lee: Mummy can't come for us. [*brightening*] Father will. [*They look scared as John, Penny, Bridget, Mark and Tim enter from right.*]

Penny: Hello! [*She goes up to the children, who are clinging together for courage.*]

John: Don't you belong to the Gipsy encampment?

Lee [*defensively*]: What if we do? We're doing you no harm.

John: I thought you were in some sort of trouble and we could help.

Becky [*starting to cry again*]: They've moved our caravan on, and we don't know where they have gone.

Penny: Why aren't you with your Mum?

Lee: Our mother was ill, we had to fetch the doctor. He went in his car, and we walked back.

Bridget: The doctor will know where they are. Come back to school with us, we'll ask Miss Thompson to phone him.

John: My Dad is coming to fetch me, he'll drive you back to the caravan.

Becky [*doubtfully*]: He wouldn't want to give us a ride in his car. Nobody want us. [*She begins to cry again.*]

Mark [*timidly*]: Have a sweet. [*He hands round a bag of toffees. All the children take one.*]

Tim: Hadn't we better hurry? We'll be late for the Nativity Play.

Lee: The what Play?

Bridget: The Play we have at Christmas about Jesus.

Becky: Who's Jesus?

John: He was a King born in a stable with all the animals.

Lee: Don't know any King. We live in a caravan and are always moved on. We have only our Dobbin. He's a donkey.

Bridget [*suddenly*]: But so was he, moved in the middle of the night. His mother rode a donkey.

Becky: Was he one of us?

Lee [*scornfully*]: Course, not, bet his father didn't sell pegs and things at the market like Dad.

John: His father was a carpenter and sold things to people who needed them. He wasn't rich.

Bridget: Why don't you come and see it? We have a lovely tea afterwards, and presents from the tree.

John: We'll find out where your caravan is. Don't worry.

[*Lee and Becky look doubtfully at each other.*]

Penny [*holding out her hand*]: Come on, it's cold out here. Your mother will be better soon.

Lee [*still looking troubled*]: It's our Mum. She's going to have a baby. I don't want to worry her.

John [*excitedly*]: You are like the Christmas story! [*He ticks the facts off on his fingers.*] A baby, you've been moved on, you have a donkey, your father works with wood. It all fits.

Lee: You mean he really was one of us?

John: Sure he was.

Becky: Then let's go to see him.

[*All the children run off the stage right, pulling the gipsy children with them.*]

SCENE II

[*The Nativity Play is mimed. The gipsy children can be seen standing at the side of the stage watching intently. At the conclusion, a reading or a carol is sung, allowing time for the stage to be set for Scene III.*]

SCENE III

[*An old mattress is in the corner left, while another mattress with a pile of covers on it is opposite right. Between the mattresses at the back of the stage is a table. On it stands a hurricane lamp, some cups, a tin and some plates. A young gipsy is heating some milk over a primus stove. His wife is lying on a mattress left nursing a baby.*]

Mother [*anxiously*]: You are sure the children are safe? It's dark now.

Father: The farmer's wife said the children were watching a play at the village school, and someone would bring them back. It was very kind of her to give us this milk, wasn't it?

74

Mother: Yes, and the eggs too.

Father: I think I can hear a car coming along the lane. [*He goes to the right side of the stage and looks out.*] Yes, the children are running across the field. [*He waves.*]

[*Lee and Becky run in from the right of the stage. Each carries two parcels wrapped in gay paper. They both try to speak at once.*]

Becky: This is for you. [*She gives her mother one of the parcels.*]

Lee: I've one for you. [*He gives his father a parcel.*]

Father: Hush, both of you. You'll wake the baby.

[*Both children creep across to look at the baby.*]

Lee: Is it a boy? [*His mother nods.*]

Becky: He's sweet.

[*Father has unwrapped the scarf, which he winds round his neck.*]

Father: How did they know I needed one?

Lee: I don't know. We have a present too, but not to be opened until Christmas Day.

Mother: Just look! [*She unwraps a blue woollen shawl, which she winds round herself and the baby.*] Lovely and warm. What was this play about?

Becky: It was about a King who was one of us.

Father: We've never had a king in our gipsy tribe.

Lee: His father made wooden things like you. He was quite poor.

Becky: He had to move on in the night. His mother had to ride a donkey like Dobbin.

Lee: It really is true. He was one of us.

Becky: Except for the shepherds and the angels.

75

Mother: Didn't you say a shepherd told the doctor where to find us?

Father: Yes, the shepherd told the doctor where to find us.

Lee: There you are. [*He puts his present on the table. Becky does the same.*]

Becky: What about the angels?

Lee [*confidently*]: They'll come.

Mother: You've both had an exciting day, I think you should have a rest.

Father: I hear Dobbin. He wants his supper. [*He goes to the left side of the stage, then comes back.*] It's starting to rain and it's cold. I'll bring him in, shall I?

Mother: Yes, there's room for him by the children.

[*Becky and Lee unroll their mattress, pulling the covers over themselves and lie down.*]

Becky [*starting up*]: I hear the angels singing. Listen!

[*Off stage the remainder of the cast sing softly 'O Little town of Bethlehem'.*]

Lee [*triumphantly*]: I said they'd come. It's a magic night.

Mother [*looking at the baby*]: There does seem to be some magic in the air tonight.

[*The children lie down again, smiling happily, as father comes back for the lamp.*]

Father [*quietly to his wife*]: The singing is coming from the church down the lane. I think it's some choir boys. I saw them going in earlier.

Mother: Hush. It's angels to the children. They are almost asleep. Bring Dobbin in, dear, out of the cold.

[*The carol continues to the end as the mother looks down at the baby.*]

Curtain

TAD'S TALE

A Christmas story for miming or acting, by Lilian Boucher

This piece, which has been performed in mime with an adult Narrator in church and also broadcast as a play on local radio, lends itself to imaginative production. Directions have not therefore been given for moves. Breaks have been indicated where carols may be sung, and are included. Please note that the last three lines were used in the radio version only, and can be omitted if the Narrator is young.

Cast:

Narrator
Tad, a shepherd boy
Shepherds (up to 8 in number)
Angel
Attendant angels, who may be dancers
Choir
Mary and Joseph
An optional group of 'audience' to sit around the Narrator's feet, reacting appropriately to his story.

Carol: 'O come, O come, Emmanuel'

Narrator: Yes, I was out on the hillside
The night that it happened,
Taking care of the sheep, with the men.
Right bad tempered, they were too,
I remember quite clearly.
All grumpy and jumpy,
Didn't really want to be bothered with me
A young boy of ten,
Keeping night watch
For the very first time.
And quite scared, I can tell you!
  They sat round in the firelight
Grumbling and mumbling to one another.

Even snapped at old Ben when he stirred.
But scarcely a word
Was spoken to me,
As I sat there miserably
Hoping the night would soon come to an end,
But it didn't. It dragged on and on,
    Until, all of a sudden
Ben stiffened and growled,
Ears upright, fur bristling!
Then, the mumbling-grumbling stopped!
The shepherds looked anxiously round —
Stared through the darkness —
Waiting — listening. For what?
I didn't know. I just sat there petrified,
Holding my breath.
Wishing like mad I were back
In the crowded city below,
Not there, on that bleak hillside.
    Then, up through the still air,
Came the faint sound of rustling,
The sharp crack of dried twigs,
And — the terrified bleat of a lamb!
    'Ach! Another unwanted stray
Trapped in the thorn below.
Go, get it lad. You're younger than I am.
And be quick about it!' Matt ordered.
    Well, scared though I was
I daren't disobey.
So I picked up my stick
And walked most unsteadily out of the firelight
Into the darkness.
Stumbled down to the bush in the hollow
And, after a struggle, set the lamb free.
    And a trembling, wee thing he was.
Frightened like me, I've no doubt,
Of the chilly black night
And the shadowy hill.
So I wrapped him carefully round with my cloak,
And spoke to him gently,
Until in the end
All his cries and shivering stopped.
And fluffy and warm,
He snuggled against me.
And I felt less lonely,
I'd found a new friend,
And christened him Zak.

And you know, it was then,
When I held him tightly,
I stood up to make my way back to the men,
That I suddenly felt less afraid,
And found I could stare at the night,
And the hillside around,
And the sky overhead
Where the stars shone so brightly.
Especially the new one,
That hung like a great, glittering diamond
So close to the city.
   Where had it come from?
Why was it there?
Was it an omen as some said? I wondered.
Had it made the shepherds all seem so uneasy?
'Cos they certainly were.
   I felt myself shiver
Through cold, more than fear though!
And I whispered to Zak,
'If we don't hurry back
To the fire and the men, little lamb,
We'll be frozen. So come on, let's go.'
   And then, holding him firmly
I struggled up to the top of the slope,
And had only just reached it,
And stopped to lift him a little bit higher
As my poor arm was aching,
When everything happened!
   The hill glowed all around me.
The sky seemed to catch fire,
And burned and blazed with such brilliant light.
That I tell you, I stood there amazed
With my mouth wide open!
   Then, from out of the brightness,
An angel appeared
All shimmering and white!
And the shepherds — they flung themselves to the ground
And covered their faces in fright!

Carol: 'While Shepherds Watched'

But I didn't! Oh no!
Clutching Zak tightly
I stood there and stared,
While the Angel said quietly,
'Do not be afraid.

79

I have come to bring
To you and all men
Great and glorious news.
For tonight, in David's town below,
A child is born,
A saviour who is Christ the King.
And you will find him
Lying in a manger
Wrapped in swaddling clothes.
Go down and worship him'.
  As I stood there watching
The Angel rose, but then,
With a rush and rustle of glittering wings
A host of others came crowding around.
And there seemed to be Angels everywhere,
All shining and white,
And the air was filled with the sound of their singing.
  'Glory, glory, to God on high,
And peace on earth, to men,' they sang.
Over and over and over again.
And the shepherds scarcely uncovered an eye!

Choir: 'Angels from the realms of glory', first two verses.

But I — yes, you're right —
I stood there spellbound, watching and listening.
Until in the end they just vanished from sight.
And all the bright lights faded and died.
And we were left there, on that dark hillside,
To wonder if all we had seen and heard
Was real or only a dream.
  It seemed like a dream,
And for several minutes nobody stirred.
Then Ben trotted over and sniffed at my cloak,
And the shepherds stood up and rebuilt the fire,
And spoke of strange things — of
Prophets, prophecies, palaces, kings,
A saviour, the promised Messiah.
I didn't quite understand what they meant —
I was only ten at the time, after all —
But I realised something exciting had happened,
And full of impatience,
My fears all forgotten
I tugged at Matt's hand.
'Oh do, *do* stop talking,
And let's go down into town, like the Angel said
And find that new baby!' I cried.

Matt didn't push me aside
As I half expected he might,
But growled, 'Steady, Tad, steady,
We're all just as ready as you are
To go down and find him,
Only — we're older and wiser
And can't help wondering why
A baby, especially one born to be king
As the Angel said,
Should lie asleep in a manger
Instead of a bed in — ' He broke off
As he noticed my bulging cloak
And asked me quite sharply,
'What are you hiding away under there, lad?'

'The lamb I pulled out of the thorn.
Oh please, *please* let me keep him,
You said he was only a stray,
So, I've made him my friend
And called him Zak.
And I'd like him to see the new King
When we go.
So come on, Matt, let's hurry.
The fire's blazing brightly,
You've no need to worry
That wolves will attack
While we're gone. So — oh
Come on, Matt, let's go!'

I pulled at his hand and tried
To drag him away,
But he shook himself free,
And, no doubt surprised at my boldness,
Said crossly. 'That's no way to talk
To your elders and betters.
A short time ago you had nothing to say,
We thought you were tongue tied!
But now — what a change!'
Well, he was right about that, as you know.

And he stooped down to pick up his crook.
But he must have noticed the look on my face.
For he straightened and said less unkindly,
'There's no need to wait for us, Tad.
Take the lamb and go on ahead.
Make your own way to town,
And search for the place
Where the baby lies sleeping.

Some stable maybe.
Though why, is a mystery.
We'll follow you down
Just as fast as we can, so —'
　'Matt, you can't send the boy on his own.
He's afraid of the night,' cried Dan,
And the others agreed.
　'No, I'm not,' I quickly declared.
Though I still was, a bit.
'I'll set off right away.
And don't worry yourselves about me,
I shan't be alone
I have Zak.'
　As I said this, I left them
And once more fumbled my way down the slope.
This time shouting back,
'I'll see you all later, in Bethlehem,'
　And I fancied I heard someone call
'God speed you, lad',
As I stumbled on blindly.
Maybe, they weren't such a bad lot of men
After all, I decided.
　But when I reached the rough track
That led straight into town,
And heard Ben's shrill bark
And the rattling clatter of stones falling down,
And realised they weren't far behind,
I gripped the poor wriggling Zak
Even more tightly, and ran.
Yes, I could run in those days!
I slipped and tripped from time to time
It is true. But nevertheless, I ran on
And not one bit afraid of the dark,
Or the night,
Or the shadowy hill.
You see, I'd suddenly made up my mind
I was going to be
The first of the shepherds
To find that new baby.
So I ran on and on without stopping,
Right down into Bethlehem.

Carol: 'O little town of Bethlehem'

　Nothing stirred in the still, sleeping city.
Not a soul was in sight
As I dashed past the scattered white houses,

And down the dim alleys and roadways
So hustling, bustling and busy by day,
But so empty and silent by night.
   I had no idea where to go.
I just rushed heedlessly on
Till I found myself in the Market Square,
And there, breathless and aching,
I stopped. I just had to.
And sat on the ground
With my back to a palm
And grumbled to Zak, 'It's not fair,
When the Angel told us the baby
Would be lying asleep in a manger,
He didn't say who the manger belonged to,
Or where we should find it!'
And then I suddenly realised *I KNEW* —
In the cattle shed
At the back of the inn
Close to Sam's house.

   You see, I'd remembered
That, when we'd been playing there,
That afternoon, I'd seen two weary travellers,
A man and a tired-eyed woman riding a donkey,
Turned away from the inn itself,which was crowded
And had been all day,
And taken round to the shed behind.
And I was sure it was there, in that shed,
I should find the baby
Lying asleep in the manger,
Just as the Angel had said.

   Full of excitement I sprang to my feet
And, forgetting my tiredness,
Dashed over the Square,
Up the old street that took me to Sam's house,
Turned round the corner,
And there stood the inn —
Completely in darkness.
No-one was awake!
I couldn't believe it.
Had I made a mistake
And come to the wrong place, after all?

   Well, there was only one way to find out.
So I stepped through the arch
Where the travellers had gone,
And then knew, without doubt, I was right!

Because through the cracks in the cattle-shed door
Shone yellow glimmers of light.
   I hurried over the yard
And with shaking fingers, lifted the latch.
And shall never, never forget what I saw
In the soft, shaded light,
As I opened the door
And tiptoed inside.

   The ox and the ass in the corner
Quietly munching their straw
A patient donkey beside them
And my travellers —
No longer anxious and weary —
But smiling and happy,
Bending over the manger
Where, I could see,
As I stepped further forward,
A tiny baby,
So pink-faced and crumpled,
Lay fast asleep in the hay.

   I went to the woman and whispered, 'Lady,
Is — is he the newly-born King,
The saviour the Angel spoke of?'
And she whispered back softly,
'That, I can't say,
But I do know he's special,
He's mine, and his name will be Jesus.'
   'I'm Tad,' I told her, unfastening my cloak.
'And he's Zak, a stray lamb
I took out of the thorn bush —
'Er — may he see Jesus, as well?'
   'Yes, Tad,' she replied.
   So I lifted him up and said,
'Look, here is the baby I wanted to find
Before Matt and the others.
And today is his birthday.
His very first birthday.
So, when I go back to the sheep, little lamb,
I shall leave you behind as a present.
For I've nothing to give him but you, Zak.'
I remember, I ruffled his warm woolly curls rather sadly.
   But then — do you know?
While I stood by the manger,
Watching him sleep,
The baby suddenly opened his eyes

Just for one minute,
And gave me a beautiful smile!
As if to say, 'Thank you,
I'm glad that you came, Tad.'

Choir: 'He smiles within his cradle'.

Surprised and delighted
I smiled back and whispered,
'I'm glad that I came, too.
But now, I must go.
Goodbye, little King. I shall never forget you.'
    Then I settled Zak down
In the hay round the manger
And said to the tall, bearded man,
'Keep the lamb as a birthday present for Jesus.
I'd better go back and take care of the sheep now.
They've been left all alone,
As the rest of the shepherds are on their way here
To look for the baby.
Maybe I'll meet them,
And then I can tell them
Just where he is.'
    But I had hardly finished what I was saying,
When the scuffle of feet,
And the sound of low voices
Came over the yard. 'Oh!
They've found us already.
They're here now,' I cried
    And before I could reach it
The shed door burst open
And Matt and the others
Came rushing inside — like a whirlwind —
And without seeing me,
They went straight to the manger,
Bent over the baby asleep on the hay.
Stood silent a moment,
Then, thrilled and delighted,
They huddled together and murmured excitedly,
'Say, this baby —
He must be the Christ Child,
The Saviour, the King,
The long promised one
That the Angel spoke of!'
    Then they bowed down before him,
And fell on their knees
And praised God for his coming,

While the tall bearded man looked thoughtfully on,
And the woman mysteriously smiled.
    And that's how I left them,
To make my way back
Through the still, sleeping streets
Of the city of Bethlehem, up to the hill.
To take care of the sheep
For the rest of the night
On my own. No, I wasn't afraid.
    And as I sat there in the firelight alone,
I thought of that baby asleep in the manger,
And wondered just why
An Angel had come to tell us of his birth,
And nobody else. Well, as you know,
We were only rough shepherds,
We weren't important.
So was it because we were up on the hillside
Awake at the time that it happened?

    No, there must be a much better reason that that
I decided. Then realised the truth —
Or at least, so I thought.
And sprang to my feet
And cried out aloud, 'Oh, but
I know,
I know,
I know,
Why he came!
He came to tell *us*
So that *we* can tell *others*
That Jesus
    The Christ Child
    The Saviour, is born.
Is born for us all in Bethlehem town.
And take them to greet him,
On this, his first birthday.
And I will! Oh, I will!'
    Straightway I set off down the hill
In the oncoming dawn
The words echoing round me,
'Go — go and tell others,
Tell others, tell others.
That Jesus
    The Saviour,
        The Christ Child is born.
            That Jesus, the Christ Child, is born!'

Nearly forty-three years have gone by since that night,
But I can still remember it —
So clearly.

Carol: 'Good Christian men, rejoice.'

Note: In the original production, the carol 'In the Bleak Midwinter'
was sung at the end of the play, after the line 'That Jesus, the
Christ Child, is born!' During this the final tableau was formed
with the whole cast. Actors stayed in place for the offertory
prayers, which followed, and left in procession during the singing of 'Good Christian men, rejoice.'

The carol 'He smiles within his cradle' is to be found in *Congrega-
tional Praise* and also in *The Oxford Book of Carols.*

AWAY IN A WIGWAM

An unusual Red Indian nativity sequence with carols, written (with apologies to H.W. Longfellow) by Mr. E. Bowyer, head of Medlock Junior School, Manchester.

The action takes place in a Red Indian village somewhere in North America.

SCENE 1 *Red Indians are displaced by the white man.*

Choir: 'Land of the Silver Birch' (*Singing Together*, BBC Publications, 1978)

> [*Children are dancing around the totem pole, watched by adults including their chief. Enter Fleetfoot, a breathless messenger. Dancing stops, all gather round him.*]

Fleetfoot: Brothers are approaching across the great plain. Look, there are their messages of smoke. [*Everyone looks as he points. They keep looking as suitable music is heard.*] Look! Here they come.

> [*People crowd together to watch. Enter a group of Red Indians with their chief. The two chiefs exchange greetings.*]

1st Chief: How! Why are you come?

2nd Chief: Our land has been taken from us by the pale-faced settlers. We have come to find a new home in your country.

1st Chief: We greet you in peace. You may live here with us beside the great river and build here lodges for your people.

A squaw: Come, we will give you food. [*Some newcomers move away with villagers.*]

88

Brave (Joseph): I must find a place for my squaw to rest. She is tired and her baby is nearly due. [*He goes to one or two wigwams, but they are already full.*]

Choir: 'Nobody cares at all' (*Carols for Children*, Southern TV)

Villager: Here is an old birch-bark lodge where she may lie. It has not been used for years and birds and animals have taken shelter here. See, I will drive out Kahgahgee, the raven. [*He shoos the bird away. Kahgahgee flies away, squawking.*]

Brave: Thank you, my brother. May the Great Spirit reward you for your kindness.

Choir: 'Away in a wigwam' ('Away in a manger' with first line altered), and/or 'Bring a light' (*New Horizons*, Galliard/Stainer & Bell), 'Jesus, Jesus, rest your head' (*Carol, Gaily Carol*, A & C Black)

SCENE 2 *A message from the Great Spirit*

[*The villagers return to their activities. Some of the newcomers join them. Suddenly they hear a voice from the totem and turn to look.*]

Voice: I am come from the Great Spirit,
From the Lord who ruleth all things,
He who formed the earth and blue skies,
He who made the lofty mountains
And the forests with their tall trees

Pointing upwards to the heavens,
Upwards to the starry heavens;
Made Ahdeek the mighty reindeer
And Adjidaumo the red squirrel,
Gave them mosses for their breakfast
And the nuts which they can gather.

He has sent me with a message,
Sent a message for his people,
For the warriors and the fishers,
For the hunters and the trappers,
From the oldest to the youngest,
To the young men and the maidens:

'I have seen how hard you wrestle,
Wrestle hard and wrestle fiercely
With the spirit who brings evil,
Mitche Manito, Spirit of Evil.
I myself will come to help you,
I will send my son to save you,
From the bosom of his father,
From the mansions of my heaven.
Even now he lies among you.
You shall worship at the cradle
Of my only son, my first-born,
Prince of peace for everlasting.'

Choir: 'Huron Indian Carol' (*Merrily to Bethlehem*, A & C Black)
'In the fall of winter' (*New Orbit*, Galliard/Stainer & bell)

SCENE 3 *The child in the wigwam*

1st Squaw Where shall we find the child?

1st Brave: Does he lie in the chief's wigwam?

2nd Squaw Does he ride in a canoe of gold?

2nd Brave: Does he lie in the white man's town?

Choir [*speaking*]: From his home beyond the forest,
Where the sun is everlasting,
From the presence of his father
He is born in humble bark lodge,
Living here with earthly parents
Who have come to dwell amongst us.

3rd Brave: He must be with one of the new families who have taken refuge here. [*All begin to search.*]

3rd Squaw: This is where he lies! See the light of peace upon his face!

Choir: 'A little child on the earth has been born' (*Oxford Book of Carols*) and/or 'O, ru, ru, ru' (*Singing Together*)
'Mary had a baby' (*Carol, Gaily Carol*)

SCENE 4 *The warriors*

Choir: [*speaking.*] See the warriors with their faces
    Fearsome all with gleaming war-paint,
    Tomahawks held at the ready,
    Scalping knives with blades all gleaming,
    Sharpened on the tribal whetstone,
    On the stone where down the ages
    Many braves their knives have sharpened.
    See how stealthily they travel —
    Through the long grass they are creeping.
    Not a movement shows the places
    Where they glide with snake-like motions,
    Glide and slide with snake-like motions,
    Anger gleaming on their faces.

    Oh, how long must war and bloodshed
    Be the thing in which you glory?
    Must you always hurt your brother,
    Ever seek to do him mischief?
    Will you learn the way of friendship,
    Learn the way to peaceful living,
    Learn to treat all men as brothers,
    Doing all things for their good?
    He has come, your friend and saviour
    He a chief who bears no sword.
    He, the Prince of Peace, is with you,
    Born a child to be your Lord.

Choir: 'A baby in the manger laid' (*The Musical Salvationist*) or
    another carol of coming to the manger, such as 'Come, leave
    your work' (*The Galliard Book of Carols*, Stainer & Bell)

1st Warrior: We must go and find this baby.
    We must hasten to his cradle.

2nd Warrior: Let us go in peace to see him,
    Leave our tomahawks behind us,
    Leave our bows here with their arrows
    Safely resting in their quivers.

    [*They go to the lodge.*]

1st Warrior: Wonderful counsellor, we come to learn of you.

2nd Warrior: Mighty God, we come to praise you.

3rd Warrior: Everlasting Father, we come to be your children.

4th Warrior: Prince of Peace, we come to serve you in peace.

Choir: 'Coldly the night winds winging' (*Faith, Folk and Nativity*, Galliard/Stainer & Bell)

SCENE 5 *The Hunters*

Choir [*speaking*]: By the shores of Gitchee Gumee
    By the shining Big Sea Water,
    See the hunters softly moving,
    Stalking slowly through the greenwoods.
    See their arrows at the ready,
    Arrows sharpened for this purpose
    By the ancient arrow-maker,
    He who fashioned heads of sandstone,
    Arrow heads of chalcedony,
    Arrow heads of flint and jasper,
    For the hunting of the reindeer
    And Pezhekee, the great bison.
    See the ripple of their muscles
    And the laughter on their faces
    As they go with stealthy footsteps
    To the bank beside the river
    Where, to drink the crystal water,
    Wabaso the little rabbit
    And the deer come running daily.
    See the hunters softly moving,
    See their arrows at the ready.
    Do they know that close beside them,
    Peaceful, sleeping in a wigwam,
    Lies the baby, prince of all men,
    Who is born to be their leader?

Totem: Oh, you hunters, softly moving,
    Leave your arrows and your stalking,
    For your Lord, the mighty Spirit,
    Has revealed to you his purpose:
    He has sent his son among you.
    You will find him in a wigwam.

1st Hunter: Let us go to search and find him.

2nd Hunter: See, a light from yonder wigwam!

3rd Hunter: Here's a rabbit fur to give him. [*Holds it up.*]
It will keep him warm in winter.

[*They come to the lodge.*]

Choir: 'The holly and the ivy'

SCENE 6: *The Chiefs*

Choir [*speaking*]: Mighty men of strength and valour,
Mighty men who know all wisdom —
Know the lore of all their people —
They are set to be our leaders,
They are set to rule our village.
Great are they and we must serve them.
They have heard news of his coming
From the bosom of his Father —
Lord of earth, a tiny baby,
Lying in a humble wigwam
In a birch lodge in the village.

See, they come to do him homage,
Bow before the humble wigwam
Where the king of earth lies sleeping.
Here is big chief Oskonoto.
He brings gold mined in the mountains
Far beyond the big sea water,
Where the pine trees reach to heaven.
And the mighty chief Grey Eagle,
Bringing moccasins of leather
Brightly beaded by his people,
People skilled whose clever fingers
Decorate with bead and feather
All the garments of the village.
Morning Cloud, chief of the Sioux,
Is the third and final chieftain.
He brings precious gum from pine trees,
Gathered from the mighty pine trees
Growing in the distant forests
Far beyond the big sea water.

[*The chiefs approach and present their gifts.*]

Choir: 'To Jesus, from the ends of the earth' (*Faith, Folk and Nativity*) and/or 'What shall I give to the child in the manger?' (*Carol, Gaily Carol*)

Choir [*speaking*]: So we leave you with this message,
Leave you with this word of counsel
As we reach the festive season,
As we come again to Christmas.
Jesus Christ is not the saviour
Only of Red Indian people —
He loves folk of every nation,
Black or white, redskin or yellow.
He invites you now to meet him,
Bids you now to hail his coming,
Asks you once again at Christmas
To find a place where he can dwell
In your heart, where he will bring
Peace, joy, happiness and love.

Choir: 'On Christmas night all Christians sing' and/or 'Good Christian men, rejoice'.

Note: *Carols for Children* was published by High-Fye Music Ltd., 10 Denmark Street, London WC2H 8LU, and *The Musical Salvationist, Vol 49*, from Salvationist Publishing Supplies Ltd., Judd Street, London WC1. If these are not readily available, other carols may be substituted. As this was a full-scale school production, many carols were included. Should it be necessary to reduce the number, that sung first in each group is the most appropriate to retain. Note also that the singing and speaking choirs need not be the same.

THE LAND OF SHADOWS

A dramatised story by Nigel Sustins, for service or assembly.

Narrator: A reading we often hear at Christmas is this one from Isaiah in the Bible:

'The people who walked in darkness have seen a great light; they lived in a land of shadows, but now light is shining on them.'

Here is a story that helps us to understand what Isaiah is saying. In a land where many people lived, both rich and poor, there was darkness. The Wise Men of the land said that this was because there was no King. There was a palace with a throne, but no one had sat on it for as long as anybody could remember. People were sad and angry because the sun never shone. The rich had darkness all the time. All sorts of horrible things would happen in the dark.

The Wise Men sent out a letter to be read at every street corner:

Messenger: We must find the right man to be King. When he sits on the throne, the darkness will lift. Anyone who thinks he may be the King, or who knows who the King is, should report to the palace immediately.

Narrator: Soon the would-be Kings began to arrive. The first was a very rich man, with many servants and treasure chests.

Rich Man: The King must be a wealthy man. I am the richest man in all the land. So I must be most fitted to be King.

Narrator: He sat down on the throne, but the land stayed as dark as ever. He lived in the palace for three days, then all the poor people from the city came to the palace and pulled that Rich Man off the throne in their anger.

The next one to arrive was a very fat man.

Fat Man: The only way to enjoy life is to eat as much as you can. I am the fattest man in all the land. If I am King, everyone will be happy and the darkness will lift.

Narrator: The Fat Man moved into the palace with his mounds of food and cooking-stoves. He sat on the throne and his servants fed him. But it stayed dark. After three days, the hungry people in the city grew very angry and attacked the palace, dragging the Fat Man off the throne.

After this a very beautiful woman arrived.

Woman: What you need is a Beautiful Queen, not a King at all. I am the most beautiful woman in all the land. I will drive the darkness away with my good looks.

Narrator: She sat down on the throne and her servants did all they could to make her even more beautiful. But it stayed dark. After three days, all the sick and ugly people in the city came to the palace and drove the woman out.

The next man to arrive came with the loud sounds of a musical band.

Music Man: Music is the most important thing in the world. It can drive away the darkness. We'll sing and make music, and things will start to happen.

Narrator: The Music Man sat on the throne with his band gathered about him. Music filled the palace. But it stayed just as dark as ever. This time people didn't wait three days. They could only stand the noise for one day. They all rushed into the palace and threw out the musicians. Then they called the Wise Men together.

Voice 1: Why can't you find the right King?

Voice 2: None of these have done any good.

Voice 3: You must do something or we'll pull the palace down.

Narrator: The Wise Men talked together and tried to sort things out. As they were talking, a young boy came in with his parents.

Wise Man: What do you want?

Boy: I've come to try the throne.

Wise Man: But you're only a child. What can you do?

Boy: What we need is love between all the people in the land. Just bothering about ourselves is no good. If Love is King, there will be light and peace for everyone.

Narrator: The Boy went up to the throne and sat down. At that moment the sun shone through. The Wise Men were amazed and all the people in the city ran towards the palace to see what had happened.

Wise Man [*to boy*]: Now what will you do?

Boy: I will spend my life spreading the news of love to everyone. Then the darkness will lift, not only from the sky but from people's hearts, too.

Narrator: Isaiah has this to say:

'A child is born to us; a son is given to us.
And he will be our ruler.
He will be called: "Wonderful Counsellor, Mighty God,
Eternal Father, Prince of Peace".'

[*Pause*]

In the dark Kingdom, the sun gives no light.
Men are sad, full of fear, lie and cheat and fight.
Who will bring gladness back to this dark land?
Who will come with peace like a lantern in his hand?

Many take the praise which they think is theirs alone.
Many take the crown and themselves sit on the throne.
Do they have the answer that brings the land's release?
No, none of them can last; none of them brings peace.
Wealth and food and music, beauty, pass away.
All have failed to light the sky again with day.
Only one may sit on the throne of man's great need:
A Child without a crown, who brings love instead of greed.

A SLIP IN TIME

A girl who is bored with Christmas is the central figure in this play for older juniors/middle school children, by Roberta Bell

This play was written for performance in a church with a side aisle and chancel to the left, the pulpit on the right and the way out to the vestry to the left of the main chancel, so the stage directions are given accordingly. It can, of course, he adapted to a church with a different layout. It was also possible for the characters who entered from the vestry or the side chancel - [Mary, Joseph, Innkeeper, Servant and Herod] to double as modern schoolchildren in the first scene. Admittedly, Mary had to be a very quick-change artist!

Cast:

Miss Johnson, a present day English school teacher
Charlotte, a school girl
Other schoolchildren - at least three or four

Mary
Gabriel
Joseph
Innkeeper
Shepherds, at least three
Balthazar
Melchior
Kaspar
Servant
Cherubim (optional)
Narrator

Before the play begins the audience are asked to join in singing the following verses of 'In the Bleak Midwinter': Verse 1 at the beginning; verses 2 and 3 (of the five verse version) after Herod's exit; and verse 5 after the final tableau is formed.

Audience: 'In the Bleak Midwinter' (verse 1)

[*The Narrator takes his place at the lectern, where he remains throughout.*]

Narrator: 'A Slip in Time'. The play takes place in Israel today and in Palestine at the time of Christ's birth. Scene 1: Outside the Church of the Nativity at Bethlehem.

[*Enter Miss Johnson and Schoolchildren from side chancel, Charlotte last.*]

Miss Johnson: Come along, children! This is the church built over the site of the place where Jesus was born. Of course, there was only a stable here then and it was all very primitive, but people wanted to worship at this place and so they built this church here. People from all Christian traditions come and worship here. Charlotte! Will you stop lagging behind!

Charlotte: Well — I'm bored.

Miss Johnson: Bored? *Bored*! For goodness sake, child, this is the chance of a lifetime, to be here and see the actual place where Jesus was born —

Charlotte: But I *am* bored. I think all this Jesus stuff is rubbish. I don't believe any of it.

Miss Johnson: I don't understand you. You've been sulking during the whole of this trip. Why did you come, if you think it all so beneath you?

Charlotte: Anything's better than being at home. Going to church with Mummy and Daddy and singing carols and visiting sick children in hospital — yuk!

Miss Johnson: I think it's time you pulled yourself together, young lady, and started counting your blessings. Now come along, children! Angela - Sarah, will you stop squabbling — and, Tracey, stop chewing and come along!

[*Miss Johnson and the other children go down the main chancel and out to the vestry. Charlotte dawdles, mimicking Miss Johnson.*]

Charlotte: Tracey, stop chewing and come along! Now, children, this is the entrance to the church ... silly old idiot ... it's all rubbish anyway ... [*She goes to follow the others but trips and* *falls heavily.*] Ouch! Ooh, that hurt! [*Sits up slowly and looks round her, bewildered.*] What happened — where — hey! It's all different! How come I'm in a — a *garden!* [*Enter Mary from vestry.*] Hey, miss — could you tell me — [*Mary ignores her as she comes to the front of the chancel, picking flowers.*] All right, *be* like that — but I don't think she even saw me! [*Charlotte continues to stare at Mary, who is now at the foot of the pulpit, still picking flowers.*]

Narrator: Once upon a time there was a girl called Mary who was in love with a man called Joseph. One day Mary was in a garden picking flowers when she saw a figure surrounded by a bright light ...

[*Gabriel rises in the pulpit. Mary steps back, startled.*]

Gabriel: Come over here, Mary, and listen to me. [*Mary is very frightened.*] Don't be afraid. I have a message for you. God has chosen you over all women to be the mother of his son. You must go home and talk to Joseph because you must be married very soon. [*Mary turns to go.*] Mary, when your baby is born he is to be called — Jesus.

[*Gabriel sinks down into the pulpit. Mary goes out to the vestry, past Charlotte, still ignoring her. Charlotte stands up.*]

Charlotte: Goodness, I wonder what all that was about — who were they? And what weird clothes! This place doesn't look a bit like it did this morning. I wonder where the others are?

[*Voices are heard off, calling 'Charlotte' but she doesn't hear them and wanders off to sit in the front pew below the pulpit.*]

Narrator: Mary went home and told Joseph what the angel had said, and they were married. While Mary was expecting her baby, the Government said that everyone must return to the town of their birth so that they could be taxed. Joseph took Mary to Bethlehem. They had a long way to go and travelled for several days.   Scene 2. At the Inn.

[*Mary and Joseph enter from side chapel. Joseph sits Mary on the pulpit steps and goes up the right side of the chancel, 'knocking' on inn doors. The Innkeeper enters from the vestry and comes down to the front of the chancel on the left, as Joseph comes down that side, still knocking. Charlotte comes up from front pew to the centre of the chancel.*]

Charlotte [*looking at the audience*]: Heavens, what a crowd — and everyone jabbering away in different languages! I wish I knew what was going on .. If only someone would speak to me, so that I could find out where I am, but nobody even seems to *see* me! [*She turns and sees Mary.*] Gosh, there's that woman I saw in the garden ... she looks as if she's going to have a baby!

[*Charlotte leans against the choir stalls near the pulpit steps as Joseph approaches the last 'inn'.*]

Joseph: Oh, landlord, I was wondering if you had room for two ...

Innkeeper: Go no further, mate! There's not an inch of room anywhere here. My wife and I have even given up our own room. This taxing is all very well — a nice boom — but what about when it's all over, when you've all gone —

Joseph: My wife! The baby! I don't know what to do! This is the last inn — have you no room anywhere?

Innkeeper: We-ell, you can sleep in the stable, I suppose. At least it's dry, even if it does smell a bit.

Joseph: Thank you, thank you! At least Mary can rest there while I look round. Come, Mary.
[*Joseph collects Mary and they follow the Innkeeper to the vestry. Charlotte comes centre.*]

Charlotte: Stable? No room at the inn? Mary, expecting a baby? It's just like that old rubbish Miss Johnson's always on about. But that's only a yarn and this is for real ... I think. Well, I'm real and they're real, but we don't seem to be able to connect. Mary ... Joseph ... Jesus ... Oh, it's all rubbish! I wish the others were here. I'm going for a walk.
[*She goes down to front pew below pulpit.*]

Narrator: That night Mary's baby was born in the stable: a little boy, and they called him Jesus. Mary laid him in the straw in the manger because she had nothing else. And the animals standing round kept him warm.

[*The first tableau is formed during this reading. Joseph enters from vestry, carrying the manger which he places on sanctuary steps, centre, and stands beside it. Mary enters with the baby in her arms. She lays him in the manger and kneels beside it. Mary and Joseph sing 'Away in a manger', with help from the rest of the cast if their voices are not strong enough. Then they go out to the vestry, taking the crib with them.*]

Narrator: Scene 3. The Hills outside Bethlehem. On the hills around Bethlehem there were flocks of sheep watched over by shepherds.

[*The Shepherds enter down nave from the back of the church and sit round their 'fire' on the chancel steps. Charlotte comes up, unnoticed, and leans against the choir stalls again, watching.*]

One group was gathered round their fire, eating their supper. Suddenly they heard singing and saw before them an angel in a bright surrounding light ... They were very frightened.

[*Gabriel appears in the pulpit.*]

Gabriel: Don't be afraid. I have come from God and I bring you good news. Your long-promised Saviour has come. Down in the town of Bethlehem a baby has been born. He is the Son of God. You must go and worship him.

1st Shepherd: You give me a feeling of great peace. I believe you. But how shall we find this baby?

Gabriel: You will find him with his parents in a stable. He will be lying in a manger.

2nd Shepherd: Come on, let's go.

[*Gabriel disappears into pulpit. 1st and 2nd Shepherds get up and go down chancel to vestry.*]

Shepherd Boy: I'm coming too, father! I'll bring the baby a lamb!

[*He gets up and runs after the others.*]

Charlotte [*coming centre*]: That ... man told them to go and worship a baby! Old Johnson should really see this lot! They all got up, left the sheep and went off to worship a baby! Some people will believe anything. Still, there were those singing voices ... and that light ... How dark it is now! I wonder ... I must have stepped through time somehow ... I wish I could go back!

[*She turns and sits disconsolately in the choir stalls on the right.*]

Narrator: Scene 4. The Kings at Herod's Court. At about the time that the shepherds were hearing of the birth of Jesus there were, living in different countries in the East, three wise men who were like kings to their people. They had worked out by charts made from the stars that a great king would be born in Bethlehem in Judea. They set off from their own countries to take gifts to the new king. They met each other on their journey and decided to travel together. The kings were very rich and carried rich gifts.

[*Kaspar comes from the front pew on right, Melchior from front pew on left, Balthazar from back of church. They meet at the front of the nave, bow to each other and go up to the chancel steps. Herod enters from vestry, followed by his Servant, and sits on the altar rail, centre.*] Their journey took them to the palace of Herod — the King of Judea — where they thought the baby would be born.

[*The Servant comes forward as the Kings mount the chancel steps.*]

Kaspar: Good day. We are looking for the new baby king that has just been born hereabouts. Can we see him please? We have brought gifts for him and have come a long way.

Servant: I know of no new baby king! I will ask my master.

Balthazar: We wish to see the new king who has just been born. Isn't he here in the palace?

Herod: I am King here, and my wife and I have no sons. Who told you of this new king?

Melchior: We have seen his star in the East and it led us here. Truly, sir, a new baby king has been born. We have brought gifts and travelled a long way to see him - we followed the star by day and night!

Herod: You got here by following a star? How amazing. Well, maybe this star will guide you to the exact place where the baby is and when you find this young king, come back and tell me where he is so that I, too, may take him ... gifts.

Kaspar: Yes, we will do that. We will go onward now.

[*The Kings bow and go back down the chancel and out by the side chancel.*]

Herod: Slave, follow them! I want to know where there is another king in my country! [*Servant hurries after Kings.*] A baby he might be, but babies grow up. I am King here and there will be no *other!* [*Draws sword and goes out to vestry, brandishing it.*]

[*Audience sing verses 2 and 4 of 'In the Bleak Midwinter'. During verse 4, 'Angels and archangels may have gathered there', Gabriel descends from the pulpit, collects Cherubim, if any, from side aisle, and they go and take up their places at the centre of the entrance to the sanctuary. The rest of the tableau is formed as the Narrator describes it.*]

Narrator: Scene 5. In the Stable. Mary sat by her baby who was in the manger. [*Joseph and Mary come on with manger, and take up positions, as before.*] Joseph stood beside her as the shepherds came in and knelt in wonder. The shepherd boy has brought a lamb. [*Shepherds enter from vestry, and take up positions on far side of tableau.*] The kings come in, one by one, and offer their gifts.

[*Kaspar, Balthazar and Melchior come from the side chancel and go up, one at a time, to lay their gifts at the foot of the manger and take up their positions on the left. Charlotte watches them intently as they go past.*]

Narrator: They have found their new baby king, not in a rich palace, but lying in the straw in a humble stable.

Charlotte [*coming to centre of chancel steps*]: Now I've seen it all! Three kings going into that stable, together with those shepherds. And there's that star! It's been in the sky for days, not just at night. Right over the stable it's stopped ... I never saw a star so bright, or so close ... Could it really be that that old story is true ... that Jesus really was born on this earth, in a dirty old stable ... that Jesus is real ...? I'm going to see! [*She is about to rush up to the tableau, but swings back.*] But I wish I had a gift like them!

[*Charlotte then creeps up to see the picture of the Nativity. Audience sing last verse of 'In the Bleak Midwinter'. Charlotte runs to the front of the chancel and leaps onto pulpit steps.*]

Charlotte: It's true, it's all true!. That Christmas story I've always thought was rubbish! Oh, I wish Miss Johnson could be here! Oh, wait till I get back and oh, oh, I can't wait to tell them all - but will they ever believe me?

KEEPER OF THE INN

A moving play for nines to thirteens, by Cynthia Woodward

Characters:

The Virgin Mary
Joseph
Joses, the Innkeeper
Rachel, his wife
Jessica, a girl
Samuel, a boy
Gabriel
Angels

Nicodemus ⎫
James   ⎬ shepherds
Philip   ⎭
Simeon, a shepherd boy
1st Reader
2nd Reader
3rd Reader
Choir

Properties:

Chairs. Light table. Bag of money. Rugs. Wood for fire. Box for manger (not essential). A screen is useful if there are no curtains.

This play is intended for the nine-to-thirteens age-group, though there need be no upper age limit.

PROLOGUE

1st Reader: And it came to pass in those days, that there went out a decree from Caesar Augustus, that all the world should be taxed.

And all went to be taxed, everyone into his own city.

And Joseph also went up from Galilee, out of the city of David which is called Bethlehem, because he was of the house and lineage of David, to be taxed with Mary his espoused wife. [*Exit*]

SCENE 1

[*A room in the inn at Bethlehem. On stage chairs and a light table. Enter Mother and Jessica. Mother carrying rugs.*]

Mother: Well, we still have one room left to ourselves, Jessica. [*Both sit as she speaks*] I don't remember the inn ever being as crowded as this. No more mats for anyone to lie on, and these rugs are hardly fit for use. Help me mend them for that last family who arrived. [*Both start mending*]

Jessica: Father says he can't take many more people. He'll soon have to close the doors.

Mother: He's taken in more now than we've room for. But I couldn't be the one to turn them away. Some have had to journey three and four days to get here.

Jessica: What will happen when we've filled every bit of space, and can't get one more person in?

Mother: We'll see, Jessica. Let's hope it doesn't come to that.

[*Enter Innkeeper and Samuel, a young boy. Innkeeper carries a bag of money.*]

Innkeeper [*crossing to table, and putting bag on it*]: It's come to it now, Rachel. People packed in every space, all ready to pay well for food and a mat to lie on, or a rug for covering. Listen to this. [*Rattles bag*]

Mother: I wish we didn't have to make money from other people's misfortunes, Joses.

Innkeeper [*Sitting down, and starting to count money*]: If I didn't someone else would.

Samuel [*Standing by table, helping father*]: I don't think anyone else will come tonight. It's getting dark. I saw Simeon and his brother a few minutes ago going up the hills to mind the sheep. I'd like to go with them one night. Could I, father?

Innkeeper: You've no sense of your position, boy. A son of mine minding someone else's sheep!

Samuel: King David watched sheep. Simeon says it's wonderful in the hills at night, and James, the old shepherd, says you're close to God up there.

Innkeeper: Signs and wonders! I've never had much use for such talk.

Jessica: Isn't God in the hills then, father?

Innkeeper: About as much there as here.

Jessica: Could God come to this inn, father? I thought God could come anywhere.

106

Innkeeper: That's enough, now. Get on with what you're doing and not so many questions.

Jessica: But, father —

Mother: That's enough, Jessica. Of course God could come to this inn, or anywhere else for that matter, but there's far too much selfishness and unkindness about for him to want to come. [*Examines work*] Well, that's the best I can do. If anyone else arrives, there'll be no covering for them.

Jessica: P'raps we could give them our cloaks. Could we, father?

Innkeeper [*wearily*]: No Jessica, we could not. I wouldn't give my good cloak to King Herod himself, nor yet to the Roman Emperor.

Samuel: Don't you like the king or the emperor?

Innkeeper: I do not.

Mother: Be careful, Joses. Suppose someone heard!

Innkeeper: Then I would take the consequences. There's too much bowing and fawning in Israel.

Samuel: Wouldn't you want to bow even to the king and the emperor?

Innkeeper: I would not. I would wish to bow to one Being only between heaven and earth, and that Being is God. And I would want my son to do the same.

Samuel: Yes, father.

Jessica: But first you said God wouldn't come here, and now you say you'd bow to him. How —?

Innkeeper: Be quiet, both of you, and let's have a little peace.
[*a knock*]

Mother: Run to the door, Jessica. See who it is. [*As Jessica goes*] I hope it's not more people for lodgings or they'll be unlucky.
[*Jessica returns*]

Jessica: It's a man and a girl. They want to stay the night. They've come seventy miles.

Innkeeper: Say we're sorry, but there's no room. They're too late.

Jessica: Father, I *can't.*

Innkeeper: You *can't?*

Jessica: No, father. I'm sorry, but I can't.

Innkeeper: Do as you're told before I get angry.

Jessica: Please, father, don't ask me to.

Innkeeper: I'll tell them myself, and you can explain yourself later.

    [*Exit. Others turn towards door, listening.*]

Innkeeper [*just off stage*]: I'm sorry, but there's no room. [*Pause*] No, it's not a question of money. [*Pause*] I realise you're exhausted, and I can see your wife shouldn't be dragging round the streets in Bethlehem. I wish I could have helped you but perhaps you'll find somewhere else. [*Returns*]

Jessica: Father, how *could* you?

Mother: Jessica, calm yourself. I don't know what's the matter with you. Don't scold her, Joses. She hardly knows what she's saying.

Innkeeper: But she *does* know what she's saying, and she's right. I hated saying no to them. The girl wasn't much older than Jessica. And her face! So drawn and pale, and yet it had a sort of light to it. I can't explain.

Mother [*trying to calm him*]: It wasn't your fault we had nowhere, Joses.

Innkeeper: I sent her away cold and exhausted, to goodness knows what nightmare. I sent her away and, Rachel, she thanked me and tried to smile. I don't know what I've done.

Jessica: Let me go after them, father. They could have my corner. I'll sleep in the stable.

Innkeeper [*hopefully*]: The stable? Haven't we let it, Rachel?

Mother: Why, no, of course not, it's not fit ...

Innkeeper: Then the travellers could have it. They'll be able to rest and it's out of the cold.

Mother [*realising its possibilities*]: And there's plenty of hay for a bed, and the animals are docile enough.

Innkeeper: Then off you go, Jessica. After them as quick as you can.

Jessica: Oh, *yes*, father! [*Runs off*]

Mother: I'm glad we could help. I don't remember seeing you and Jessica so upset before. I must take these rugs to the last family that came. There won't be any for these two travellers, but I'll take over a lamp and some warm food.

Innkeeper: Thank you, Rachel. I'd be glad if you'd see what you can do for them.

[*Exit mother with rugs.*]

Innkeeper [*musing*]: No, I never saw such a face as hers. I don't like to think of a slip of a girl like that with no covering against the cold. Samuel!

Samuel: Yes, father?

Innkeeper: Run quickly. Get my cloak and take it to the stable.

Samuel: Your cloak? But father, you said you wouldn't give it even to the king.

Innkeeper: And nor would I. Now run along. [*Exit Samuel*]

Innkeeper [*calls after him*]: My best cloak, mind. Not my old one. [*To himself*] No, I never did see such a face.

[*Curtain, or exit Innkeeper.*]

Carol: 'A Virgin Unspotted', sung in whole or part, but omitting 'shepherd' verses.

2nd Reader: And Mary brought forth her firstborn son, and wrapped him in swaddling clothes, and laid him in a manger because there was no room for them in the inn.

And there were in the same country shepherds, abiding in the field, keeping watch over their flocks by night.

SCENE 2

[*Hills near Bethlehem. A shepherd, James, stands looking into distance, keeping watch. Another, Philip, tends the fire. A young shepherd, Nicodemus, enters with Simeon his brother, a shepherd boy. Simeon sits on his bundle. James joins the group.*]

Nicodemus: Peace be to you, James, and to you, Philip. Did you think we were never coming? We set out early enough but Simeon here had to stop and talk to young Samuel.

Simeon: He said he'd ask his father if he could come to watch the sheep with us one night.

James: He'd be welcome, but I don't think his father would agree to that, Simèon.

Nicodemus: I've explained the Innkeeper wouldn't want to humble himself to mix with us shepherds, he wouldn't want Samuel to, either. He's a proud man, though there's much good in him.

Philip: He'll certainly be getting plenty of travellers at his inn today, and all paying well, I've no doubt. Is the town still crowded?

Nicodemus: Full, and more arriving every minute. And many worn out with the journey.

Philip: Registering and taxing! All these Roman orders. It doesn't matter what hardships people have to suffer because of them.

Nicodemus: It'll be a different story when our promised Saviour comes. I pray I live to see the day.

James: So do we all. But it's time we were taking watch again, and young Simeon here will be getting tired.

Nicodemus: Right! Off to sleep with you, Simeon. James and Philip, you rest as well. You were watching before we came. I'll take a turn now. [*He walks a little way, then stands. Philip and Simeon lie down. James sits by the fire.*]

Simeon [*to James*]: But I'm not tired, and I can't sleep with the stars shining down on me. I've never known them so bright. They're even brighter than the lights of Bethlehem.

James: So they should be, Simeon, seeing God made them.

Simeon: James, when God does send our Saviour, will he make much difference?

James: If men will let him. Now, try to sleep, or you'll be tired later.

[*James lies down. Silence. Softly as from a distance comes the refrain 'Gloria, Hosanna in Excelsis' from the carol 'Ding Dong, Merrily on High'. Simeon sits up, listening.*]

Simeon [*shaking James and Philip*]: Listen! I can hear something. It sounds like voices singing and it's getting nearer.

[*The shepherds are now all listening in wonder. As the refrain is repeated, and the singing reaches its climax, Gabriel comes in, with angels, hands as in prayer. They stand in group, Gabriel in front. Note: they may alternatively be represented by a strong light and voices offstage. Shepherds kneel, covering faces. Gabriel raises arm, as in blessing.*]

Gabriel: Fear not. For behold, I bring you good tidings of great joy, which shall be to all people. [*Shepherds raise heads, still half-fearful*] For unto you is born this day, in the city of David, a Saviour which is Christ the Lord.

And this shall be a sign unto you. Ye shall find the babe wrapped in swaddling clothes, lying in a manger.

[*The refrain 'Gloria in Excelsis' is repeated three times, each time more faintly as the angels go off. A pause. Slowly the shepherds rise.*]

Simeon: Who were they? Where did they come from? What did they mean?

James: They must have been angels, surely. Bringing such tidings I could hardly understand. But they came from God all right.

Simeon [*ashamed*]: And I was so frightened.

Nicodemus: We all were. My eyes are still dazzled, and my ears still ringing. A Saviour, did he say, born in the city of David?

Philip: That's here in Bethlehem. And the angel meant us to look for him. 'Ye shall find the babe,' he said. But where shall we look first?

James: He said the baby would be in a manger. That would mean a stable. There are many stables in Bethlehem.

Nicodemus: There can't be many with a new-born baby.

James: Come on. let's look till we find the one where he's lying. For didn't the angel say this baby was our Saviour, Christ the Lord?

Simeon: Let's hurry, then p'raps we'll be first there. [*As they go*] Look, how the way to Bethlehem shines. The stars are gleaming as though the angels were still there, and lighting the way for us to our little lord.

Carol: 'O little town of Bethlehem' (2 verses) Tune - English traditional melody.

3rd Reader: And it came to pass, as the angels were gone away from them into heaven, the shepherds said one to another, Let us now go even unto Bethlehem, and see this thing which is come to pass, which the Lord hath made known unto us.

And they came with haste, and found Mary and Joseph, and the babe lying in a manger.

SCENE 3 *The Stable*

[*Mary is seated centre, the child in her arms, Joseph at her side. If there are no curtains, Mary and Joseph can have been concealed behind a screen until now, to avoid having them walk on. The Virgin sings her lullaby.*]

Mary: sings 'The Coventry Carol'.

Carol: 'O Come, All Ye Faithful'.

[*During the singing of this carol, the shepherds come in singly, bowing, then kneeling. Then comes the mother, lastly Jessica and Simeon. All bow before the Holy Family, then kneel.*]

Carol: 'Little Jesus, sweetly sleep' (*sung by Jessica and Simeon*)

[*Enter Samuel and Innkeeper, but not on stage. They may be at side of church or hall, but must be clearly seen.*]

Samuel: Isn't it wonderful, father, all that Simeon told me about the angels telling the shepherds our Saviour had been born. And then finding him here in our stable! But I forgot — it's signs and wonders, and you never had time for such things.

Innkeeper: Don't be disappointed to find it was an old man's dream -- a boy's imagination — eyesight playing a trick in the darkness.

Samuel: But would all the shepherds have the same dream? And they knew where to find the baby. Mother says they couldn't have imagined that.

[*They start to move towards the stage*]

Innkeeper: I'd like to believe. There's certainly something special about the baby's mother. But I'm sure there's some perfectly reasonable explanation for all that's supposed to have happened. Yes, I just need a little time to think, then I'll be able to explain it all.

Samuel: I'm glad you're coming to see the baby anyway. Mother's there, and Jessica, and the shepherds. [*They mount stage from the front*] Look! Everyone is kneeling. Shall I kneel too? Oh, I forgot again. You said you would never kneel to any being between heaven and earth except God, and I mustn't either. So we'll just stand, shall we?

[*Innkeeper and Samuel are now on stage, their upright posture contrasting strangely with the adoration of the worshippers.*]

Carol: 'What child is this?' Tune 'Greensleeves'.

[*During singing of first two lines, Samuel looks round at scene and up at father. Slowly, head bowed, he drops on one knee. For a second the Innkeeper remains erect, then, during singing of third and fourth lines of carol, with dignity and humility he kneels and bows low among the shepherds before Jesus. The carol should be timed so that the triumphant last four lines, starting 'This, this' come immediately after his kneeling.*]

[*The angels (if used) now come in and group themselves round the holy Family. They should not come in before the Innkeeper kneels. The Choir sings the rest of the carol.*]

Carol: 'Silent Night'

[*During the singing of this carol, the characters of the play remain in tableau. If there are no curtains, they should remain so, if possible, until the audience or congregation has gone. If this is not possible, they leave in procession.*]

WINTER

by Noel Connell

The low sun gleaming through November branches,
Stark silhouettes of woodland dank and bare;
The morning mist, the sudden grip of winter,
The blink of warmth at noon, the days that were.

The sunny hours and burnished fall are over,
The calendar's full circle nearly told,
And nature's hand grows firm and bleak and quiet,
And age begins to shrink before the cold.

Cosy the hearth and warm the indoor laughter;
Our compensations are this time of cheer,
Time to remember, time to make beginnings,
Time for the promise of another year.

A poem for Assembly, by Claude Holmes

FIRE RISK

A reply to a friend's letter—
apparently dictated in his office
and beautifully typed

Thank you for yours of December First.
I note that you are not keeping Christmas this year,
That you are, however, no Scrooge
   and suitable organisations will benefit —
   your secretary will tell me which.
I note your view that Christmas is for kids —
   enough for you to sign the charitable cheques
   and choose a card of decorous design
   (with a printed signature, of course)
   to offer your best wishes to your many friends,
   while you depart for your winter cruise.

I note the reasons for your view of the occasion.
To you it is the realisation
of a salesman's dream of Paradise,
this celebration of a birth that might —
   or might not —
have taken place in a warm and scruffy stable
   noticed by no-one
   but a handful of shepherds
   and a harassed housewife taking time off
   from behind the bar.

I further note —
Your remark that it is good for business —
   tinsel spending and a boom in the off-licence,
   and that the fir tree with its ruined roots
   is a pagan relic brought here by a German prince;
and that you object to the candles as an added fire risk.

I agree ... Christmas *is* a Fire Risk.
  Divine fire which darkness cannot douse
  and therefore dangerous.
  Light illuminating the shadowy corners
  so easily by-passed in the dark.
  Fire glowing through the pretty wrappings —
  frightening fire
  threatening to consume heart and soul —
  Light uncontainable in two thousand years
     despite the bombs,
     despite the plagues,
     despite the floods,
     despite the old man who will die in pain, and the
     empty cot and the failure and the bitterness.

Since you have borrowed the Birthday
to celebrate whatever you wish to celebrate,
   please find enclosed an invitation to the party.
No compulsion — no charge —
but you will be welcome
to warm your hands in the light of the candles.
Then go out and sign your cards yourself.

THE WANDERING STAR

by Tom H. Jones

'Is this the place where the Christ Child is?'
Said the Kings to the Wandering Star.
'For this is Rome, and fit for the home
Of a new-born infant king.
See the eagles gold of the legions bold
And the glint of their gleaming helms
As the marching hordes with their burnished swords
To Caesar their tributes bring.'

But the Wandering Star, its light grown dim
In the glow of the morning sun,
Sped swiftly across the crimson sky
And gently whispered, 'On.'

'Is this the place where the Christ Child is?'
Said the Kings to the Wandering Star.
'In these desert lands with their burning sands,
Can the infant king be here?
See the chattering apes and the purple grapes
In the tents of the Arab sheiks,
See the prancing steeds, and the silks and beads
As the camel train draws near.'

But the Wandering Star, its light grown dim,
Now weaker and weaker shone;
And it moved away through the crimson sky
And gently whispered, 'On.'

'Can this be the place where the Christ Child is?'
Said the Kings to the Wandering Star.
'Can the stable meek of an inn so bleak
Be the home of a new-born King?
See the infant small in the lowly stall
With the cattle crowding round
Where the shepherds will, from the snow-clad hill,
To the child their tributes bring.'

Then the Wandering Star, its light grown great
In the dusk of the dying day,
Its journey done, stayed gleaming there
And softly whispered, 'Stay.'

THE CAROL OF NO ROOM

by Pamela Egan

In Bethlehem there was no room;
By flickering lantern light
Some poor men saw a babe in straw;
'Be welcome, child, tonight.'

Within that stable was no room
Could hold the world's new light.
For all he came — men's gift was shame,
A tomb as dark as night.

Within the grave there is no room
Can cage this living light —
It leaps forth free, to all ... to me ...
Be welcome, Love, tonight.

THE KING IS COME!

by Hilda Rostron

His reign began within a byre,
his throne, a manger poor;
shepherds as courtiers wondering stood
within the stable door.

No sceptre in his royal hand,
no crown upon his head,
but cattle fodder from the fields
for carpeting and bed.

His reign began within a byre;
amazing wondrous thing!
He still, with love, rules all the world:
Child Jesus; Christ the King.

CHRISTMAS HANDS

by Hilda Rostron

Strong gentle hands.
friendly to feel of wood;
weathered and skilled
and altogether good:
kind Joseph's hands.

Soft tender hands,
ready to soothe and ease;
homeworn and dear,
most beautiful are these:
Blest Mary's hands.

Small budlike hands,
scarcely uncurled as yet;
so frail and still,
holding in Love world's debt:
Sweet Saviour's hands.

CHURCH BELLS RINGING

A song by Dilys Wavish

Once again it's Christmas morning,
Hearts and voices raise,
Celebrate Christ's birthday dawning
With all your praise.

Chorus:
Church bells ringing, choirs singing,
In the frosty air,
Feet are winging, swiftly bringing
Men to prayer

Gather round, all join together
In a joyous band,
Hear the sound of many voices,
Through the land.
Chorus:

Let the wonder in the faces
Of each little child
Bring us peace, make all the races
Reconciled.
Chorus:

May the vision of that other
Christmas long ago
Bind us close, each man a brother,
Friend, not foe!
Chorus:

LET'S SING A SONG FOR CHRISTMAS

suggests Hilda Rostron

Let's sing a song for Christmas
of shepherds on the hill;
Let's sing of hosts of angels
carolling when all was still.

Let's sing a song for Christmas
about a stable poor;
Let's sing of kneeling Wise Men,
a baby to adore.

Let's sing a song of Christmas:
a manger filled with hay,
and of the new-born Christ Child,
born that first Christmas Day.

Let's sing a song for Christmas
and give it wings of love
to fill the sky with music
where Christ's star shines above.

(Teachers may be able to find a well-known hymn tune to which this verse can be sung.)

CHRISTMAS BELLS!

A carol to the tune
of 'Jingle Bells'
by John Kennedy

(The chorus 'Christmas bells! Christmas bells!', could be sung twice
at the beginning and end and just once after verses 1, 2 and 3.)

Chorus:
Christmas bells! Christmas bells!
Christ is born they say.
He came down to earth for us,
In Mary's arms he lay.

Angels made it known,
Shepherds came to see
The King of kings and Lord of lords
In a stable born for me.

Chorus: Christmas bells! Christmas bells!

In the inn they found no room,
In a manger he was laid,
Where the ox and ass, dumb animals,
In tribute lowed and brayed.

Chorus: Christmas bells! Christmas bells!

Wise men came from afar,
Precious gifts they brought
To the One who gave up all for us
And made himself as nought.

Chorus: Christmas bells! Christmas bells!

He came and still he's here,
Still with us to-day;
So let us put our trust in him,
The Truth, the Life, the Way.

Chorus: Christmas bells! Christmas bells!

THESE CHRISTMAS DAYS

**A carol with original music
by headmaster James A. Thomas
from Smannell, near Andover**

When the Christmas bells ring out,
Bring the news to girl and boy
Sing a song and raise a shout.
It's the time for joy.

Gather all your friends around.
To a party let them come.
Where the fun and happy sound
Means that Christ has come.

Now when the bells ring out their peal,
Over the woods and snowy fields,
Telling the message loud and clear
That Christmas days are here.

So let hearts and spirits lift
For a time of happiness.
And let friendship heal the rift.
Then our days are blessed.

Look at the gilded Christmas Fir tree,
Look at the twinkling coloured lights,
Listen to children's happy songs,
As they view the Christmas sights.

In this season's festive mood,
Let us vow to change our ways,
Let us always live the year
As these Christmas Days.

When the Christmas bells ring out, Bring the news to girl and boy sing a song and raise a shout It's the time for joy Gath-er all your friends a- round To a part-y let them come Where the fun and happ-y sound Means that Christ has come

Now when the bells ring out their pe-al Ov-er the woods and snow-y fields Tell-ing the mess-age loud and clear That Christ-mas days are here So let hearts and spir-its lift For a time of happ-i-ness And let friend-ship heal the rift Then our days are blessed

Look at the gild-ed Christ-mas Fir tree Look at the twinkling col-oured lights Lis-ten to child-ren's happ-y songs As they view the Christ-mas sights In this sea-son's fest-ive mood, Let us vow to change our ways, Let us al-ways live the year As these Christ-mas Days.

COME AND SEE THE BABY

An original carol by David Lankshear, recorder part by Jane Lankshear and piano part by Fiona Battersby

Shepherds gazing at the sky,
See your vision, wonder why
You were chosen from on high,
Come and see the baby.

Wise men in your far-off lands,
Midst the rocks and rolling sands,
Travelling with camel bands,
Come and see the baby.

Herod in your palace great,
With your soldiers stand and wait,
But the news will come too late —
You won't see the baby.

Christian people everywhere,
Will you only stand and stare?
With us all come join in prayer,
Come and see the baby.

Note: The melody line should be played by the pianist for practice, but should be omitted once the singers are secure in their part.

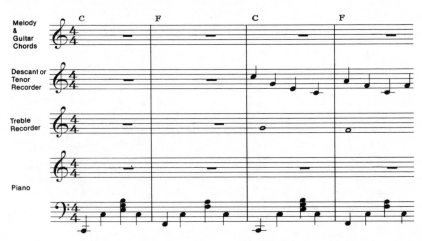

Melody & Guitar Chords: Shep—herds gazing at the sky See your vision won—der why
You were chosen from on high Come and see the ba—by.

TO ETERNITY

A Christmas song with words by
Keith Lewis and music by his daughter Amanda

Did you ever hear the story of the star
And of how the wise men came from lands afar?
Did you ever hear the greatest story ever told
When they brought the myrrh and frankincense and gold?
For the brightest star that shone that night, they say,
Came to guide those three old wise men on their way,
For the wise men from the Orient were meant to see
That a stranger, in a manger, who was born in lowly poverty,
Came to love them, really love them, dearly love them, to eternity!

Did you hear the story that they came to tell
Of the Angel who is known as Gabriel?
How he comforted the lowly shepherds that they might
Come to Bethlehem one silent Christmas night?
For, they tell, the angel said to comfort them
'There's a little baby born in Bethlehem.'
So they came and saw and knew for sure they'd all agree
That a stranger, in a manger, who was born in lowly poverty,
Came to love them, really love them, dearly love them, to eternity!

Did you hear the story how a star shone down
On a lowly stable in a little town?
How they say a donkey came to clip-clop on his way
Just to get to Bethlehem on Christmas Day?
So the little donkey saw the manger stall
And the boy, who was born to save us all,
Came to let him know he'd come to show him truthfully
That a stranger, in a manger, who was born in lowly poverty,
Came to love them, really love them, dearly love them, to eternity!

Did you hear the story that they came to tell
Of the night the Angels sang the first noel?
How a little child so meek and mild, of virgin birth,
Came to bring undying love to all on earth?
For the Son of God was born for me and you,
So with thankful hearts let's show we love him too;
For he died in pain to rise again that we might see
How a stranger, in a manger, who was born in lowly poverty,
Came to love us, really love us, dearly love us, to eternity!

Allegretto

BETHLEHEM AND BACK

A story for under-sevens
by Brian Sears

It was Christmas Eve and Mrs Bear had cooked scrambled eggs for tea. 'Everything else is a scramble getting ready for tomorrow so that's how I'll do the eggs,' said Mrs Bear. Timothy Bear didn't mind at all. He liked scrambled eggs and anyway his thoughts were full of Christmas — the first Christmas. For a year or two he had particularly liked the idea of animals being near to baby Jesus in the stable and now at the tea-table he was thinking about it again.

'I wonder what it was really like in that stable at Bethlehem,' he said aloud as Mr Bear passed him the salt.

Timothy must have wondered very hard indeed because all of a sudden there was a whirring sensation inside his head and a feeling that he was tumbling backwards through time and space. It ended with a tiny bump. At first Timothy kept his eyes tightly shut but his snout sensed strong smells — not altogether unpleasant but certainly strong. His ears heard confused animal conversations.

When Timothy opened his eyes, to begin with it didn't make much difference. It was very dark. Slowly his eyes became used to his surroundings. A little starlight came through gaps in the roof. Timothy was huddled in a corner with three other animals who didn't seem in the least surprised that he was there. It was quite easy, too, to follow their animal chatter.

A cow was having her bad-tempered say. 'What a lot of fuss', she moaned, mooing moodily. 'We can hardly move and now we've been invaded by humans. It was bad enough when there were only two but just look at all those shepherds.' There was a sympathetic braying and one or two embarrassed bleats. 'And that's not the worst of it,' continued the cow. 'Who's ever heard of a cow scratching for food on the floor before? We're no chickens. Look! My food tray has been taken over by a human calf!'

Timothy Bear was now quite sure where he was, but he was still surprised when he heard himself speaking up with his usual strong gruff voice. 'Steady on! Don't you realise who that baby is? It's Baby Jesus who will become a great king.'

'Stuff and nonsense,' retorted the cow. 'Listen to our furry friend. A king will never be born in our stable. It's too draughty for a cub, let alone a king.' She lowed a laugh hard and bitter.

A donkey took over from the cow and Timothy was glad he spoke more gently. 'A King, you say. We don't care much for kings here, anyway. They cause trouble with their fighting and their armies.' 'This King is different', said Timothy, feeling better. 'He's not a king just for soldiers and winning wars; he will be a king of love and of peace. In fact,' went on Timothy, nodding at the donkey, 'when he grows up he will ride into a city on one of you to show that he comes peacefully, and not on a war-horse.'

'We could do with a king like that,' brayed the donkey. 'I think I'll go over to have a closer look.' He edged over towards the cow's food tray. The baby's mother and father smiled, making room, and the baby's tiny hands stretched to tickle the donkey's ears.

There was a sad bleat at Timothy's side. 'I'm too small for anyone to ride,' sobbed a sheep. 'I'm not much use at all.' 'Don't think like that,' said Timothy. 'When that baby grows up he's going to tell a story about a flock of sheep. One of them, just like you, gets quite lost and Jesus, as the good shepherd, goes looking for you everywhere until he finds you.' The sheep was cheerful again. 'I should like to be found by Jesus,' she said. The stable was quiet.

'Yes,' said Timothy Bear. 'He won't only look for sheep, but donkeys, bears, humans — even grumpy old cows.' The animals made gentle noises of pleasure and when Timothy Bear looked the cow had joined them and had quite lost her miserable look.

Timothy saw no more of the stable. Again he seemed to be spinning through time and space and with the tiniest of bumps he was back at his own tea-table.

'Yes, I wonder what it was really like as well,' Mr Bear was saying, balancing the scrambled egg on top of a piece of toast.

'But I know,' said Timothy. 'I've just been there.'

'Don't be silly,' said Mr Bear. 'You've been sitting here all the time.' Timothy knew it was no good to argue. It was hard to sort it out himself.

Much later, when Timothy Bear went to bed, he was still thinking of the grumpy cow that cheered up. He took off his bow-tie and something floated down and landed in his slippers. He bent down to pick it up. It was a piece of hay.

TIM-IN-THE-BOX

Another Timothy Bear story
for younger children,
by Brian Sears

Timothy Bear was wondering which part he would be given in this year's Nativity Play. Two years ago he had been one of the children of Bethlehem, last year he had been a shepherd and this year he would like very much to be a king. Two Sundays before Christmas Sunday, Timothy's teacher announced what was going to happen. 'We'll be doing our play in the church in front of your mums and dads,' she said. 'Claud, I want you to be Joseph and this year, Linda you'll act the part of Mary, the mother of Jesus.' Everyone enjoyed the thought of Linda doing that.

'Timothy,' went on Miss Thorn, causing an excited tingle inside Timothy's fur, 'I wonder if you'd be one of the kings?' The delight on Timothy Bear's face was answer enough. 'Which king would you like to be.' 'The one who carried the gold, please,' he answered promptly. He wasn't very good at saying frankincense, and myrrh always sounded a bit sad.

When he arrived home, Timothy couldn't remember who were going to be the shepherds or the innkeeper's family. He couldn't even remember the other kings! Mrs Bear was delighted for him. 'I'll make a golden cloak for you and then we'll make a crown with jewels in it.'

Busy Mrs Bear found time to do as she said. It truly was a splendid cloak. Timothy helped her with the crown. 'What shall I carry?' asked Timothy, as Mrs Bear curved card round his head to make sure the crown would be the right size. Mrs Bear thought for a moment. 'There's the tin that Grandma's chocolates came in for your birthday. It's empty now and we could cover it with gold paper.' That would be the next job.

'Why did the king bring gold as a present?' asked Timothy as he cut out some coloured paper shapes for the jewels. Mrs Bear smiled at yet another question and because she knew what the answer would be. 'He wanted to give the best and most precious present he could.' Timothy was thoughtful, sticking on the sticky shapes. Mrs Bear wasn't surprised that quite a long time went by before he spoke. 'I would like to bring presents to Jesus,' Timothy said slowly.

'Well, there's room in Grandma's tin, you could put something of yours inside,' said Mrs Bear. 133

Timothy Bear bounced upstairs. He remembered a spare 10p piece in his jacket pocket and there was that tractor that had lost its wheel. They would fit Grandma's tin. As he came downstairs again he stopped. The king had given gold because it was the best thing he had. A spare 10p piece and a broken tractor didn't match up to that. He went back to his bedroom and searched again.

When Mrs Bear next saw Timothy she could scarcely see his face, he was so loaded with presents to give. There was his favourite card game, a jar of honey that he kept in the drawer for hunger emergencies, the 10p piece and a £1 note that he had saved, his Action Bear and an almost full box of chocolates. 'They'll never go in Grandma's tin,' chuckled Mrs Bear. Timothy had already thought of that. 'We could cover that box the envelopes were in,' said Timothy. Mr Bear had brought it home from work.

'That's a good idea, Timothy, but I wonder still if you're giving the best and most precious present of all.' 'What else is there?' asked a puzzled Timothy Bear and it took quite a while for Mrs Bear to explain.

The Church was crowded on Christmas Sunday. In the hall at the back the children were dressed and ready in good time. Then the play began. Linda and Claud looked really tired after their long journey; the innkeeper shook his head sternly and then remembered the stable; the angels delivered their message to the shepherds so clearly; the shepherds hurried so much that one tripped up the step into the stable. Then it was time for the kings to make their way slowly down the centre of the church. Many of the congregation smiled when they saw Timothy leading the way. His cloak was fit for a king and his crown shone – what could be seen of it, because in his paws Timothy carried a *huge* cardboard box covered with gold paper. It was the box the Bear family used to fetch the groceries and it was bigger than Timothy himself.

The kings reached Mary, Joseph and baby Jesus in the stable. They knelt and presented their gifts. Then everyone was in for a surprise. Instead of moving to the back to stand with the other kings, Timothy jumped up high and landed right inside his gold-covered grocery box. Miss Thorn put a hand to her mouth. Even she hadn't expected anything like this. 'You're like a Jack-in-the-box,' she whispered loudly. 'Not Jack, I'm Tim-in-the-box,' whispered back Timothy.

Pastor Hughes (NB: or 'Fr. Hughes', or 'Mr Hughes the Vicar', as appropriate) stepped forward with an even bigger grin than usual. 'Thank you for a really lovely play,' he said to all the children. 'Timothy has set us all an example. He has presented his most precious gift of all to baby Jesus. What a Christmas it would be if we all did the same! Mind you,' went on the Pastor, with his eyes twinkling and his hands trying to button up his jacket, 'a grocery box won't do for me. I'll need an oil drum!'   134

THE LITTLE CAROL SINGERS
A story for primary children
by Godfrey Cox

'Sixty pence for a bottle of scent! And then it was the cheapest in the shop!' Janet was cross. Curled up on the rug, she was counting the remains of her pocket money.

Her sister Jean on the settee looked at the few pence she had left and gave a sigh. 'You can't get anything decent for less, either.'

'I've got to buy mummy's and daddy's and Uncle Bert's Christmas presents yet, besides yours.' Janet looked at the fairy on top of the tree by the window. 'Can't you wave your magic wand and make some money for us?'

The fairy didn't take the slightest notice. She seemed content to stand there surrounded by tinsel, trinkets and the pretty coloured lights.

As Janet gazed sadly at the fairy, an old lady passing by stopped and leaned on their front gate, while she admired the Christmas tree through the window.

Jean waved to her. 'There's old Mrs Garton, look. I expect she has even less than we have.'

'She has no one to buy presents for, anyway' Janet sighed again.

'Oh, Janet' said Jean. 'I'm glad *I've* got someone to buy presents for, even if I haven't enough money.'

Actually Mrs Garton had stopped to recover her breath. She had just been to fetch her pension and it was taking her all her time to get home again. It was so cold.

Janet watched her go. Suddenly she cocked her head on one side.

'Listen!' she said. 'Carollers!'

'Fraid we've nothing to give them.'

'Jean!' Janet jumped up. 'That's what we'll do, we'll go carol singing. We're sure to make *some* money.'

'Smashing idea!' said Jean.

Everyone they called on and sang for seemed to be full of Christmas joy, and soon they had over a pound in their purse.

Then they came to the vicarage. 'The Vicar is sure to give us something,' Janet said.

'Let's find out. He might be an old skinflint.'

'Away in a manger
No crib for a bed ...'
they began and sang the whole hymn through, then the two carol

singers gave the door a gentle tap. It was opened by the Vicar's wife.

'Merry Christmas!' Jean and Janet chorused together.

'Thank you very much. Come in, will you, and have one of my home-made mince pies?'

Janet looked at Jean and Jean looked at Janet, and in they went.

The table was covered in Christmas wrappings, boxes, plates of chocolate and cream fudge, tablets of soap wrapped in fancy ribbon tied in a bow, kettle-holders, egg-cosies, pretty little shell-covered boxes; there wasn't an inch of room to spare!

'What a lot of lovely presents,' Jean whispered.

'Here you are.' The Vicar's wife hurried in from the kitchen with two plates. There were hot mince pies on each. 'What are you collecting for, then?' she asked.

Once again Janet looked at Jean and Jean looked at Janet. 'Well, you see,' Janet began, as soon as she had swallowed her mouthful of mince pie. 'We want to buy our mummy and daddy and friends Christmas presents and ... and ...'

'We've no money,' Jean finished. 'Things are so expensive, our pocket money won't be nearly enough.'

'Well, fancy!' the Vicar's wife exclaimed. 'I haven't nearly enough money to buy all the presents I need either, and I'm going carol singing for the Children's Home, so I can't get any that way. That's why there's all this mess. You see, I'm making my presents.'

'You've made these!' Janet exclaimed.

'Why, they're lovely,' Jean's eyes sparkled.

'Would you like to make your presents?'

'Oh, yes! yes!' Janet and Jean said together. 'Please!'

'Then I'll show you how to do it.'

For the next hour the two girls looked on fascinated as they watched the Vicar's wife deftly make her gifts. She showed them how to hem round the material for the kettle-holder, how to cut the egg-cosies, how to fasten shells on a box to make a jewel casket; she gave them a recipe for fudge, demonstrated how to make the soap pretty with crepe paper and ribbon and even how to make a pretty candle by pouring melted coloured wax round a string into a tin and letting it set.

Janet and Jean forgot all about their carol singing! They couldn't get home fast enough to find what odds and ends they had. They found two bars of soap and some ribbon and fancy paper, some shells collected at the seaside in the summer and an old wooden box which they cleaned up and covered with Polyfilla to stick on the shells. Then they found some sugar, butter and cocoa and started to make some fudge. They were so busy it was bed-time before they knew it.

Their mummy thought it was a wonderful idea and promised to let them go through the odds and ends basket the next morning.

'Janet and I have collected over a pound carol singing, we can use some of that,' Jean told her mummy.

'No, we can't,' said her mummy. 'That would be a bit mean when other people need money more than we do. We'll send your pound to the Children's Home.'

The next week Janet and Jean spent all their spare time making their presents as the Vicar's wife had shown them. They hadn't a minute to breathe! They spent nearly all one day making more fudge and packed some in a pretty box especially for old Mrs Garton.

When she opened the door she mumbled, 'Sorry, I can't afford to give to carol singers'.

'We're not carol singers, we've brought you a Christmas present', Jean told her, giving her the parcel. 'Merry Christmas!'

'For me? I never thought anyone would remember me.' The old lady was quite overcome. 'And I was just thinking that if I managed without eggs I might be able to afford a chop for my Christmas dinner!.'

When Jean and Janet told this to their mummy and daddy, their daddy said 'I'll tell you what we'll do. We'll fetch Mrs Garton round to have Christmas dinner with us.'

Needless to say, everyone had better Christmas presents than ever before; old Mrs Garton had never had such a happy Christmas for years – and Janet was sure the fairy on the Christmas tree winked at her.

MR PEPWORTH'S PRESENT

A story for 7s-9s
by John Escott

Mr. Pepworth had a junk shop. He bought almost anything old if he thought he might be able to sell it again or if it looked interesting.

Jimmy helped Mr Pepworth on Saturdays. He would tidy the shelves — and they were always getting in a muddle — or he would unpack parcels or unload Mr Pepworth's van. Mr Pepworth was very grateful for all Jimmy's help, especially round about Christmas, when he was busier than usual.

One day a white-haired man stood hesitating outside the shop. Then, as if having suddenly made up his mind, he walked briskly inside and over to the counter.

Jimmy, who was standing at the back of the shop, noticed the man's suit was crumpled and his shirt frayed. But he held his head high, even though he looked sad.

'I would be obliged, sir,' he said to Mr Pepworth, who was behind the counter, 'if you would make me an offer for something I shall be very sorry to part with.'

Jimmy was very curious as the man placed a long black case on the counter.

'Hm,' murmured Mr Pepworth, leaning across the counter and blocking Jimmy's view as the case was opened. 'And does it work?'

'Most certainly,' replied the man. 'Let me show you.'

Then, as Mr Pepworth stood back, the man raised something to his lips.

'A clarinet!' cried Jimmy, now able to see the man clearly.

The man noticed Jimmy for the first time. 'That's right, young man. Quite the sweetest instrument in the orchestra.'

Then he began to play the most beautiful tune Jimmy had ever heard. It made Jimmy feel as if he'd found something that he didn't know he had lost.

When he had finished, Mr Pepworth said, 'But why do you wish to sell your clarinet?'

The musician's face saddened. 'Because I can no longer find work. With so many younger men needing it, and ready to travel all over the country, no orchestra will employ a tired old man.'

138

Mr Pepworth frowned and Jimmy watched anxiously. Oh, how he wanted Mr Pepworth to buy the clarinet, even though he felt sorry for the musician. Perhaps, with lots of practice, he could learn to play a tune before Mr Pepworth sold it. Not as well as the musician, of course, but just a little tune.

But Mr Pepworth was saying, 'I'm afraid I don't get much call for musical instruments.'

'I see,' the old man said sadly, starting to put the instrument back in the case.

'Still,' Mr Pepworth went on, noticing Jimmy's interest in the clarinet, 'there might be another way for you to earn some money with it.'

'There might?' said the musician puzzled.

'As a music teacher,' Mr Pepworth said, a big smile on his face. 'Teaching Jimmy here to play the clarinet, for which I would pay you a fee. He's a good lad, always helping me around the shop yet never taking any payment for it. This can be my Christmas present to him. All right, Jimmy?'

Jimmy raced over to the counter. 'Oh, thank you, Mr Pepworth! That's great.'

The musician's face lit up with pleasure. 'What a splendid idea. We have an adventure in store, Jimmy, discovering music together.'

'And you won't have to sell your clarinet, not yet, anyway.'

And, as things turned out, the old musician never did have to sell his precious instrument. Other people came to hear about Jimmy's lessons, they too sent their children to learn, and soon the old man had a great many pupils.

As he said to Mr Pepworth when he came into the shop one day. 'You gave *me* a present as well as Jimmy.'

MRS DUFFY'S BIRTHDAY

A story for after Christmas
by Patricia J. Hunt

Peter and Sadie had been with mother to visit an old lady who lived in a flat down the street. Mrs Duffy lived alone and the children's mother always liked to visit her when she could.

'It's Mrs Duffy's birthday next week,' she said to Peter and Sadie. 'She'll be 80 years old, and I think she'd be thrilled if you each got her a little gift with your own pocket-money.'

'Her family will send her presents,' said Peter.

'No, she has no family now,' mother replied. 'They have died and she has outlived them all.'

'What about her friends?' asked Sadie.

'I'm afraid there are hardly any of those,' said mother. 'People often get forgotten when they get old, which is a very sad thing. So wouldn't it be nice if *we* acted like real friends and all bought her a present? Better still if we posted them to her, for she doesn't get any post these days.'

'OK,' said Sadie. "I've got enough cash to buy some wool, so I'll knit her a pair of warm mittens. From what I've seen, her hands look all bent with rheumatism.'

'I've got a bit of money too,' said Peter, 'but I want it for some special stamps for my collection. I've been saving for weeks and I've almost got enough money now.'

He looked glum, for he had set his heart on having those stamps. He and Sadie talked the matter over while mother prepared the tea. He didn't like to let Mrs Duffy down, but ... suddenly he had an idea.

'I know! I'll give her that super-looking book which Uncle Tom gave me for Christmas. I'm sure it cost a lot more money than I've got, so it'll be a very super present.'

The book was *Pilgrim's Progress*, and Peter had never liked that sort of book. In fact, when it arrived he hadn't even taken it from its box. He had cast it aside in disgust, still in its cellophane wrapping, and turned to more exciting presents.

'But do you know if Mrs Duffy reads much?' asked Sadie. 'I think her eyesight is very poor; she wears very thick glasses.'

'Oh, I expect she reads,' said Peter airily. 'Anyway, it'll be a very costly gift.'

Sadie thought it was more important to be given a present which you liked, rather than one which was just expensive. But there wasn't much time to discuss it, for mother had called them to tea, and afterwards she would have to work hard at her knitting if the mittens were to be finished in time. The red wool was such a warm-looking colour; she felt sure Mrs Duffy would like them.

After tea, Peter went upstairs to look again at the book. It had a stiff shiny cover with gold lettering on, and he didn't like to lift it from the box and so disturb the wrapping. Well, he just hoped that Mrs Duffy liked that sort of book.

Three days later Sadie had finished the mittens. They looked lovely and she was sure they would be a good fit. She made a neat parcel with pretty paper, and printed a small gift card. Peter got a big birthday card and put it in with the book before wrapping up his parcel.

Mother took the parcels to the post. 'I won't ask you what you've put in them,' she said, 'because I shall see Mrs Duffy on Friday and I'm sure she'll tell me.'

'What are you sending her?' asked the children.

'I've ordered a bouquet of flowers to be sent to her on her birthday morning, because I know she loves flowers.'

Peter looked a bit worried. He didn't think mother would be too pleased when she heard he had given Uncle Tom's present away.

When the children arrived home from school on the following Friday, mother told them about her visit to Mrs Duffy. The old lady had been thrilled with the mittens — even more so when she heard that Sadie had made them herself. She also sent her thanks to Peter for the book, but said that she was afraid her eyes could no longer read such small print.

Peter felt bad when he heard this. Then his mother added:

'Mrs Duffy was surprised to find you had put three packets of foreign stamps inside the book too. Of course she doesn't collect them, but she said that she'd send them to a sale where they could be auctioned for charity. You are a funny lad — why did you give her those?'

Peter was horrified. Uncle Tom must have put them in with the book, and Peter had taken so little notice of his present that he had missed them. And they would be bound to have been rare ones, because Uncle Tom knew a lot about stamps.

Peter was so upset that he told his mother the whole story. She suggested he used his pocket-money to buy Mrs Duffy something she could enjoy. Peter went straight out and bought a basket of fruit. Mrs Duffy was delighted with her second present — but Peter is still saving up for his special stamps!

THE MATCHBOX CHRISTMAS CAKE

A story for juniors
by Pamela Egan

It had been cold all term, but the second week of December was the coldest of all. Mr Small, the caretaker, shuffled round school complaining about 'the screws' in his arms and legs; the headmaster appeared in a strange shaggy pullover which his wife had been trying to give to jumble sales for years, and poor Miss Winter had to suffer more awful jokes about her name than even she could remember.

Outside Miss Winter's classroom window was a very small flower-bed containing a couple of frost-bitten shrubs. Birds came to sit on these every morning. They were very cold birds, their feathers puffed out round them until they looked like lumps of wool off the headmaster's pullover. All the children in Miss Winter's class felt sorry for the birds.

'They don't get much of a Christmas, do they, miss?' said Errol. 'We're in here having parties and doing the play and all that, and all they get is frozen worms.'

'Could we give them some bread, miss?' asked Sally. 'They could have some of my dinner,' she offered generously, spoiling it by adding, 'It's only pilchard sandwiches. Yuk!'

'I'm not sure that they'd like pilchard sandwiches,' said Miss Winter. 'But you've given me an idea, Sally. Why don't we make a Christmas cake for the birds?'

'What, with icing and all?' said Chris, who liked cooking but was more into chocolate crispy cakes than high-class confectionery.

'No, I don't think birds go much for icing. What they need in cold weather is fat and fruit and crumbs and seeds. If you all bring a little, we could make a really splendid bird cake. I'll get the fat. Can you all come tomorrow with just a little of something that you think the birds would like? Just about as much as would go in a matchbox.'

'Please, miss, at home we have central heating. We do not have matches,' said Susie earnestly. She was Chinese and sometimes found it hard to understand what Miss Winter wanted. Everyone

142

began to explain; they were still at it when the bell went. Next morning, as soon as they could, the class started to turn out their pockets. Miss Winter had brought in a big mixing-bowl and into it went the ingredients of the birds' Christmas cake.

There were several crusts of bread, more or less jammy; a mince-pie which had travelled in someone's duffle-coat and came out flattened and rather fluffy; porridge oats from Duncan, a slice of soda bread from Terry Rafferty, and a bit of very superior fruit cake from Marilyn, whose mother ran a tea-shop. Shushila, with a shy smile, tipped in one little plastic bag of yellow lentils and another of green lentils. Hussein brought a handful of knobbly yellow chick-peas. Rebecca had two brown, shiny biscuits with holes in, called pretzels. Everyone wanted to taste these and she had to promise to bring some more next day or the birds would have gone without. Chris gave a chocolate crispy cake, which was good of him; Sally gave half a cheese sandwich — she wasn't too fond of cheese either.

Then Susie came up, her face shining with pleasure. 'I talk to the waiters,' she explained. (Susie's dad kept the local Chinese restaurant and take-away.) 'All waiters have matches to light little lights under plate-warmers. All waiters give me for the birds.' She had five matchboxes. In one were plain noodles; in one, crispy noodles; in one, beansprouts; in one, bits of batter; and in one, boiled rice. There was a long pause in the mixing at this point while everyone asked questions about Chinese food and Susie talked more than she had done the whole term.

Miss Winter went to get her pan of fat, which she had asked Mr Small, the caretaker, to melt on his gas-ring, and she poured it carefully into the bowl.

Everyone stirred the bird-cake.

Then Miss Winter noticed Errol hanging back — which wasn't like him. 'I forgot to bring anything for the cake, miss,' he explained, looking miserable.

'Don't worry, Errol,' said Miss Winter. 'I've got some raisins here, just in case somebody did forget.' 'Errol brightened up, dropped them in and gave the mixture a good big stir, but he still looked sorry to have forgotten.

By the end of the morning the fat had set solid again and the class looked expectantly at Miss Winter. 'Will the birds get in the bowl for their cake, miss?' asked Terry.

'No, I thought we'd hang it in a net on that shrub outside the window then we can watch them as they eat it. Oh, my goodness.'

'What is it, miss?'

'The net, I've forgotten the net to put the cake in.' Miss Winter could have kicked herself. Her flat was too far away for her to go and collect the piece of old net curtain which she had carefully hunted out the night before.

'Miss, miss!' It was Errol. 'I could nip round to our shop and get one of the nets we sell oranges in. It's only round the corner, miss, I won't be a minute, honest.'

'Oh, Errol, what a good idea. Thank you! Mind how you go and be very quick back, and we'll put the cake out in time for dinner.'

In no time at all a beaming Errol was back, clutching a bright scarlet net. Willing hands helped to stuff it with the rather disgusting-looking mixture. They packed the net until it bulged, then Miss Winter opened the window and Chris and Duncan tied the bird-cake to a branch of the shrub. The window had barely shut again before a couple of bluetits shot across the playground and hooked themselves on to the net, pulling out goodies as fast as they could, while three sparrows, a starling and a robin hovered about underneath the branch, picking up all the bits that the bluetits dropped.

'Now,' said Miss Winter briskly, 'after dinner we're going to start doing some work on garden birds ...'

So for the rest of term the birds swung on the net and enjoyed their matchbox Christmas cake, while Miss Winter's class drew them and compared their sizes and found out about their habits. And the class party at the end of term turned into an international feast, because they all wanted to do the same thing again, but bringing plates of real food instead of matchboxfuls of scraps. So that's what they did.

'Miss!' said Sally, rather indistinctly, through a mouthful of chow mein (which she had discovered she liked very much indeed). 'Miss, do birds like anything special for Easter ...?'

CHRISTMAS HAS MANY NAMES

and Geraldine Mellor explores the meaning of some of these

The word 'Christmas', which is used by the peoples of all the English-speaking countries to describe the season during which the birth of Our Lord Jesus Christ is celebrated, is an old English name which was first employed in 1038. It was then spelt *Cristes Maesse*. It derives its origin, of course, from the two words 'Christ' and 'Mas', the latter being an English designation indicating 'feast' or 'festival'. Thus Christmas means 'Jesus Christ's Feast Day'.

In old-time English manuscripts and printed works, the following are just a few of the different ways in which the word is spelt: Christmas, Christenmas, Chrystymesse, Crystemes, Crystmas, Cristenmasse, Crismas, Cristemes, Crestenmes, Cristmes and Crystmasse, Cristmas, Crestenmas, Cristynmes, Kyrsomas, Christmass, Cristenmas, Chrystemasse, Crystynmas, Crystenmas, Cristemesse and Xtemas.

Relating to this, the last spelling of Christmas plainly shows where our title of 'Xmas' has evolved from.

Sometimes the Nativity of Our Lord Jesus is called 'Yuletide'. This is because, prior to Our Saviour's birth, the Anglo-Saxons celebrated their most important feast, that of the winter solstice, throughout December. They called this festival *geola*, meaning 'feast month'. Following the coming of Christianity, however, this pagan observance was transferred into the Feast of the Nativity. The name *geola* was preserved in the English and German languages, and is now applied to the festival of Christmas as 'Yule' in English, and *Jul* in German.

The description *Dies Natalis Domini* is one of the original Latin names for the Nativity and means 'The Birthday of Our Lord'. The other expressed, which is slightly longer, is as follows: *Festrum Nativitatis Domini Nostri Jesu Christi*, and translated gives us the phrase: 'The Feast of the Nativity of Our Lord Jesus Christ'.

The liturgical English expression for Christmas is, of course, 'The Nativity of Our Lord', which in the Welsh tongue is *Nadolig*, and in Italy is retained in the description *Il Natale*. In Portugal the designation is distinguished by the word *Natal*. In Spain we get *La Navidad*, in Greece *Genethlia*, and *Karàcsony* in Hungary.

The Ukranians and Russians speak about the Nativity as *Rozhdestvo Khrista*, meaning 'Jesus Christ's Birth'; while December 25th in Poland is known as *Boze Nerodzenie*, or 'God's Birth'. *Kaledos*, or Day of Prayer, is a Lithuanian term which is rooted in the verb *Kaledoti*, meaning 'to beg, to pray'.

In Germany, and among the Slovaks, Czechs and Jugoslavs, the word *Weihnachten* is employed and refers to the Mass, since it means 'the holy night', and the Mass is celebrated at midnight. Likewise in the Netherlands the Dutch call Christmas *Kermis*, or 'the Mass of Jesus Christ'.

But what about the name Nowell I can hear some of you say; 'what does it mean and how did it come to be associated with the birthday of Jesus?'

Well, the style is actually the English pronunciation of the French word *Noel*, and we can find it in an Anglo-Norman manuscript in London's British Museum, which dates from as far back as the twelfth century and records one of the earliest carols we know. In all probability, *Noel*, or the French term for Christmas, springs from two sources — the Latin *Natalis*, which gives us 'birthday', and the word *Nowell*, which means 'news'. Regarding the latter style, there is an old verse in English about the birthday of the Son of God in which the angel is made to say:

> *I come from hevin to tell*
> *The best nowellis that ever befell.*

Similarly, there can be few English-speaking young people who are not familiar with the words of that much loved Christmas carol, 'The First Nowell'.

Interestingly enough, ever since medieval times (from the fifth century to the mid-fifteenth century), a baby born on a day when an important religious festival was celebrated, was occasionally called after it. The most favoured of these names was Christmas, then Easter and Pentecost (Whitsunday). Nevertheless, the French names *Noel* for a boy, and *Noelle* for a girl have been preferred in recent years as an alternative to the Christian name 'Christmas'.

Natalie and its variations *Natalia* and *Natasha* denote 'the birthday of Our Lord', and so is a perfect choice for the little girl born on Christmas Day. Incidentally, *Natasha* is a popular appellation among the Russians.

Finally, Christmastime is sometimes alluded to as the 'Season of Emmanuel'. The ancient Hebrew name Emmanuel signified 'God with us', and that is the sincere message I send to each one of you this glad season. May your Christmas be filled with joy and happiness of the very best kind.

WHO WAS SAINT NICHOLAS?

Margaret Waugh looks at the stories told of this Christmas saint

Saint Nicholas, or Santa Claus as he has become known to thousands of children throughout the world today, was born in Patara in Turkey at the beginning of the fourth century.

He was very rich, as his parents died whilst he was still young, leaving Nicholas a great deal of money. This tall, thin, stately man became Bishop of a town called Myra and many legends are told about his work amongst the people of Myra and of the secret gifts he gave to those were in need.

It was the tradition in Turkey for a girl who was to marry to present her future husband and his family with a dowry, a sum of money, before the wedding could take place. Now in Myra there were three girls whose family was too poor to afford a dowry for them. The girls were sad as they would never be able to marry.

Saint Nicholas heard about their troubles and knew he must help. But he was a very shy man, so he waited until nightfall and then stole through the street of the sleeping city to the home of the three girls. He clambered up on to the roof and dropped a bag of gold coins down the chimney.

When the girls went downstairs the next morning, they found a bag of gold in one of the stockings which had been put up to dry by the fire. The next night he did the same thing and again on the third night, so that each girl had a dowry to present to her future bridegroom.

Nicholas is tne patron saint of sailors and another story tells of sailors caught in a dreadful storm at sea off the coast of Turkey.

The storm was raging all around them and the men were terrified that at any moment their ship would sink beneath the giant waves. They prayed to Saint Nicholas to help them. Suddenly there he was, standing on the deck before them. He ordered the raging sea to be calm, the storm died away, and they were able to sail their ship safely to port.

On his feast day the sailors of Bari, in Italy, still carry his statue from the Cathedral out to sea, so that he can bless the waters and so give them safe voyages throughout the year.

Nicholas is also, of course, the patron saint of all children, and during the Middle Ages, on 6th December, his feast-day, boy choristers of cathedrals, dressed in bishop's robes, used to walk around the city blessing the people. Then, with their companions, they would take over the cathedral services, except for Mass, until 28th December, Holy Innocents' Day. This practice was, however, stopped by Elizabeth the First.

Saint Nicholas was exiled from Myra and later put into prison during the persecution of his Emperor, Diocletian. The year of his death is a little uncertain, but we know that it was on 6th December in either 345 or 352 AD.

In 1807 his relics were stolen from Turkey by some Italian merchants. They are now enshrined in the Basilica named after him in the Italian sea-port of Bari.

THE TRUTH ABOUT GOOD KING WENCESLAS

revealed by Margaret Waugh

We all imagine 'good King Wenceslas', hero of one of our favourite Christmas carols, as a kind old man with bright clothes and a white beard, trudging through the snow on the Feast of Stephen, carrying his bundle of food to the peasant he had seen from his palace window. In fact we are very wrong. St. Wenceslas, the good king of our carol, didn't live to be an old man; he was cruelly murdered when he was only twenty-two years of age. The story in the carol is a Victorian invention; but the story of the king is worth recalling.

He was born in Bohemia over a thousand years ago, where his grandfather was king. The family were Christians, but his father, Wratislav, had married a princess of one of the pagan tribes who still lived around Bohemia.

When Wenceslas was just twelve his father died and, as he was still too young to become king, his mother ruled the country as regent. Wenceslas was put in the charge of his grandmother, Ludmilla, who was teaching him to be a Christian like his father. The pagan nobles in the queen's court were alarmed by this and persuaded the queen to banish Ludmilla to a distant castle. Here she was kept prisoner until one day, as she was praying in the chapel of the castle, three men sent by the queen, burst in and strangled her.

Wenceslas, however, had already learnt a lot from his grandmother and was determined, when he became king, to restore Christianity to Bohemia. He learnt to read and write, which in those days was unusual even for a king, and he had Christian priests smuggled into the palace by night to teach him more about the Bible and its teachings.

When he was eighteen he took over as king and immediately banished his mother and her pagan lords from the court. 'There is to be no more killing,' he said, and he set about to care for his people. He made sure the children were educated properly and the army adequately trained to resist invading tribes and that there was law and order throughout his land.

All was well for the first years of his reign, but Wenceslas had a brother, Boleslav, who was intensely jealous of him. The pagan lords who had been banned from court persuaded Boleslav to plot with them to murder Wenceslas.

So Boleslav invited his brother to stay with him in his castle home, pretending that there was to be a celebration to dedicate a chapel on the estate. When they had Wenceslas safely inside the chapel, the doors were locked and Wenceslas fell under their daggers. It is said that Boleslav aimed the first blow.

The people never forgot their good king and he was declared a martyr. Today, in a square named after him in Prague, can be seen the statue of a young man and beneath it, the words: 'Saint Wenceslas, suffer not us nor our children to perish.'

THE STORY OF OUR CAROLS

is briefly summarised
by Kevin J. Berry

One of the first signs of the coming of Christmas is the sound of carol-singers at your front door. You may hear a church choir or a group of young friends from down the road ... and they are all taking part in a tradition that may be older than Christmas itself. For carols were first sung when pre-Christian men knelt to pray to the sun.

They held festivals at the darkest time of the year, known as the winter solstice (around December 22), and a feature of their celebrations, which welcomed the returning light, was frenzied dancing in large circles or rings. Such dances were accompanied by loud songs and those tunes were the first carols. The word 'carol' can be traced in many European languages. Its meanings include 'a ring dance'. 'a song accompanied by a flute' or simply 'a little ring'.

One of the reasons why leaders of the early Christian Church chose to hold the first Christmas festival at the time of the winter solstice may have been in an effort to clamp down on the wildness and revelry previously associated with that season. Unfortunately the idea did not work. Ordinary people continued to sing the crude pagan songs they enjoyed. St Augustine angrily declared: 'If they must have songs, let them sing music of the Church!'

The call for Christmas music was answered in the year 129 when Telesphorus, a bishop of Rome, announced that the 'Angel's Hymn' should be sung during Christmas service. That hymn is now more popularly called 'Gloria in Excelsis'.

Many poets and composers were inspired to write Christmas music, but their efforts were as stiff and formal as the normal hymns. They were handicapped by having to use the Latin language which was understood only by comparatively few scholars and priests.

Before ordinary people could join in singing Christmas music someone would have to write carols in their own language. That someone was St Francis of Assisi. He had been much concerned that the people in nearby villages were no longer looking forward to Christmas with enthusiasm. In fact, one man had even encouraged villagers to ignore Christmas altogether.

St Francis and his friars arranged a crib scene in a tiny stable in the village of Grecchio. Villagers acted the story, animals took their traditional places in the stalls and the monks sang specially-composed Christmas words to popular tunes. Then everyone joined in the chorus as the actors and monks walked around the village, perhaps so starting the popular tradition of going the rounds carol-singing.

Latin remained in the choruses of carols, but many ordinary people could now join in with others, and sing as they danced.

Wandering minstrels adopted Christmas carols in their repertoires, but because minstrels could not read or write, many carols have differing versions. 'I Saw Three Ships' has as many as six different opening verses, one of which is sung to the tune of 'London Bridge'.

The three ships were supposed to have taken the skulls of the three wise men to Cologne Cathedral, but differing versions of the carol use the ships to carry other characters from the Nativity story.

Minstrels included shepherds and country scenes to make their carols more popular. Scenes from mystery plays inspired 'The Cherry Tree Carol' and 'The Coventry Carol'.

When Oliver Cromwell swept to power his Puritan followers criticised the humour and drama of the popular carols. In fact Cromwell so disapproved of the gaiety of Christmas that in 1647 the festival was abolished.

The carol went into a steady decline. It disappeared from the town but led a precarious existence in the rural areas where country people cherished their music, handing it on by word of mouth or by much-valued printed sheets. We owe the existence of the 'Wassail Song', for instance, to a well-thumbed broadsheet discovered in Bradford.

Yet the decline of the carol continued until well into the nineteenth century. Its critics despised the gay and lively tunes. When the composer Mendelssohn heard that one of his compositions had been used as the tune for the carol 'Hark, the Herald Angels Sing' he was very angry.

Just as many carols were on the point of extinction, a revival came. It started when two Victorian scholars travelled through small villages and hamlets, talking to the old folk and writing down the words of the old Christmas music. William Sandys scoured the Midlands and Davies Gilbert prepared a collection of carols he had found in the West Country.

In big towns and cities the mass-production of musical instruments and the formation of choirs and choral societies provided a ready market for the two men's collections of carols.

The revival of interest had been further encouraged by the publication of Charles Dickens' books *Pickwick Papers* and *A Christmas*

Carol. The books made Christmas itself much more popular and added new styles and traditions to the Nativity festival. Deep snow and goodwill to all men became fashionable themes in such carols as 'Good King Wenceslas' and 'See Amid the Winter Snow'.

Prince Albert, the German-born husband of Queen Victoria, made popular the introduction of Christmas trees and of 'Saint Nicholas' or 'Santa Claus', both to be used by writers of Christmas music.

The Victorians' enthusiasm encouraged Bishop E.W. Gilbert of Truro to try a new form of church service, a festival of lessons and carols.

In 1918 a festival of nine lessons and carols was started in the beautiful setting of King's College, Cambridge. It has continued ever since and is seen by many millions of viewers at Christmas.

The carols they hear are the very same that are sung on front door-steps all over England, and perhaps that is why the Christmas carol is so popular. It has retained a charm and dignity which means it can be sung and enjoyed anywhere, from splendid cathedrals to windy street-corners.

And finally ... a snapshot of Christmas far over the seas, where the customs are different but the message remains constant: Mary T. Standley recalls

CHRISTMAS IN MELANESIA

'A Child of Poverty is here' — so ran a printed notice among the home-made Christmas decorations outside the school dormitories. Of course, the schoolboys meant our Lord in Bethlehem, but to my husband, small son Timothy and I, spending our first Christmas on the opposite side of the world to our home, it seemed to apply to the boys also.

It was the morning of Christmas Eve and we had gone up the hill to the dormitories to admire the decoration — hibiscus, flame tree and bougainvillia, bits of coloured materials bought from the small Chinese trading boat, and poems written by the boys in honour of the Nativity. The sun was blazing down and shimmering on the sea as we received gifts of flowers or fruit grown in their own bush gardens (bananas, pineapples, pawpaw, yams, soursop, grapefruit) and we gave them little gifts such as soap, pencils, notebooks, razor blades sent by good Church friends in the UK and New Zealand.

The boys had had their breakfast, consisting of a thick piece of home-made bread (rather 'sad' because they had to ferment their own yeast from limes) and tea without milk or sugar. On Christmas morning they would have a large tin of jam to spread on their bread, as a special treat. It was then time for them to begin their various tasks which had to be completed before darkness fell — about 6.30 p.m.

Most of the preparation for the feast had been started two days earlier. A fishing party, mainly Polynesian, had brought in a good catch; the cowboys had killed a cow and prepared it; and all the vegetables — kumera (sweet potato), cassava and bananas, were ready. Three ovens of hot stones had already been cooking the above foods, cut up and wrapped in small parcels of banana leaves, and more hot stones laid on top of the parcels. Some had to guard this and supervise the clearing of the beach ready for laying the feast the next day.

We had written a nativity play and the final rehearsal was to take place in church in the afternoon. Fortunately we had Helen, the school nurse, who was able to take the only necessary female part of Mary. My sheets, tablecloths and tea-towels came in very useful for costumes, as did the church vestments and more bits of Chinese cotton.

The 'station' had to be weeded and cleaned up in honour of all our expected guests. All this was taking place on the small island of Ugi, eight miles long and three miles wide, in the Eastern Solomon Islands where my husband was priest-headmaster for almost six years, and I was a member of staff in the boys' school, once known as 'the Eton of the South Pacific'. What a contrast to an English Christmas! No snow, no lighted shop-windows, no mad rushing to and fro or even stocking-filling, no cakes, mince pies or turkey, no money, no TV programmes.

During the afternoon the guests began arriving − all the villagers from all around the island. Women with babies on their backs and baskets on their heads. In the baskets − a clean set of clothes for Christmas.

At 8 p.m. the church was full of boys for preparation for Communion and Compline, the service lasting about half an hour. During the week they had each made their confession − a truly Herculean task for the Headmaster listening! At 11.30 p.m. the real Christmas began with the ringing of the church/school bell. Up the concrete steps they came in crowds: 'like a mighty army, moves the Church of God'. Midnight Mass began for the Pawa boys, the boys of the Alangaula Junior School a mile distant who joined us, and the village people. Never had I heard such beautiful singing of Christmas hymns − all unaccompanied, for we had no piano or organ. Such an instrument would never have survived the humidity, ants or cockroaches.

After this wonderful service on this lonely Pacific Island − where we'd had to use a ciborium instead of the paten because the Kobura, the dreaded N.W. wind, had started to blow and the candles were soon out and the wafers, made by the boys would have blown away, and the altar frontal flapped like a ship's sails − we went to bed, not so the boys. They started off in their different island groups to travel round the island with their hurricane lamps to sing carols. We were awakened about every hour by groups of boys or villages singing carols at the door and we had to find a small gift for each party − a pineapple, tablet of smell (Lux!) soap, etc.

The next morning we were all up bright and early. The wind had died down somewhat − fortunately − and various soccer matches were played barefoot on the two pitches. By this time a ship had arrived and the crew also came to join us. Palm leaves were laid in

long rows along the beach, under the trees, the parcels of food were taken from the ovens, and we sat cross-legged on the ground and the feast began. We were gradually getting used to this strange food, which was beautifully cooked in the Melanesian ovens. No washing-up when the meal was over! Any spare parcels were shared by boys and villagers to eat later that night and the rubbish was thrown into the sea. Singing and dancing followed until time for Evensong, which again everyone attended; then our guests began to depart, their little lights bobbing away into the distant Bush, as some had an all-night trek to face. The staff then joined us for an English-type Christmas tea — a beautiful cake I'd managed to make when the boys found me lots of wild turkey eggs; some mincemeat my family had sent, and sandwiches of tinned corned beef.

A really Christian Christmas had just ended and it had been full of joy, peace and much love from our most lovable pupils.